bite *by* bite

bite *by* bite

100
STYLISH LITTLE
PLATES
YOU CAN MAKE
FOR ANY
PARTY

PETER CALLAHAN

WITH RAQUEL PELZEL | Foreword by Martha Stewart

Clarkson Potter/Publishers

NEW YORK

Published in the United States by Clarkson Potter/Publishers, an imprint of the Crown Publishing Group,
a division of Random House, Inc., New York.
www.crownpublishing.com
www.clarksonpotter.com

CLARKSON POTTER is a trademark and POTTER with colophon is a registered trademark of Random House, Inc.

Library of Congress Cataloging-in-Publication Data
Callahan, Peter, 1959–
Bite by bite: 100 stylist little plates you can make for any party/
Peter Callahan; [foreword by Martha Stewart]. — 1st ed.
p.   cm.
1. Appetizers.   2. Food presentation.   3. Party decorations.   4. Cookbooks.   I. Title.
TX740.C2194   2011
641.8'12—dc22   2010052626

ISBN 978-0-307-71879-2
eISBN 978-0-307-95335-3

Printed in China

Book design by Stephanie Huntwork
Photography by Con Poulos
Jacket design by Stephanie Huntwork
Jacket photography: Con Poulos (flaps and front); Melanie Acevedo (back)

1 3 5 7 9 10 8 6 4 2

First Edition

I dedicate this book
to my fabulous wife and sounding board,
JOSEPHINE,
and to my children,
HART AND JULIET,
who are constantly full of "mini" ideas
and who always support me in my food adventures.

contents

martha stewart

I HAVE BEEN WORKING with Peter Callahan for many years: first, professionally, in his capacity as contributor to many of our *Weddings* magazines as a caterer and "conceptualist," and then, personally, when he helped me mastermind several large parties at my own home.

What always strikes me about Peter is that he can think really, really big—hundreds of guests do not frighten him or make him nervous, and complicated scenarios never faze him. And while he thinks big, he delivers small, in the sense of finely constructed, inventive, creative, delicious, mind-boggling, tiny, bite-sized, ultra-tasty tidbits. The original dishes were never meant to be consumed daintily or in one bite, but can be—and are—when Peter sets out to do so.

As far as I know, he was the first to make tiny hamburgers—not sloppy sliders that drizzle down your chin, but extremely perfect, neat, colorful, beautifully formed mini hamburgers on extremely perfect buns with exactly the right seasoning and condiments. His Caesar salad is minute, yet not one flavor or ingredient, from the lemon juice to the anchovies to the egg yolk, is missing; and the service is impeccable, utilizing one of Peter's specially designed and fabricated serving pieces—in this case, a tiny, one-bite-size, turned wooden salad bowl.

Peter's inventiveness is now legendary—pastry spoons cradling caviar and crème fraîche; mini meatballs topped with a fork-swirled mound of angel hair pasta; sugary, handmade graham cracker, chocolate, marshmallow s'mores; and even mini hot dogs or macaroni-and-cheese mouthfuls—and his dishes are emulated by many, but rarely served as enticingly or as charmingly. This book is a gift to all of us, and Peter shares recipes, drink formulas, serving ideas, instructions, and even suggestions for special tools.

Now we will all be trying these great recipes, and hopefully, with as much success. Thank you, Peter Callahan!

callahan style at home

I NEVER SET OUT to shrink American comfort food. I thought of the dishes that have become my signature items one by one, and each time it was really the over-the-top reaction of guests that inspired me to make more. What began as an idea to do a silver-dollar-sized burger with a homemade bun, toppings, and all led to a mini grilled cheese. And when I couldn't find a small enough loaf pan for the miniature bread, I designed my own and had it made. When it came to serving, laying the grilled cheese on its side didn't do it justice, so I created a special tray that allowed us to serve them standing upright.

People flipped over the Lilliputian grilled cheese sandwiches. Not only were they incredibly cute, but they tasted just like the big version. Before I knew it, I was doing mini mac and cheese, mini hot dogs, and mini lasagnas, all made with top-quality ingredients that showcased flavor as much as style. The ideas flowed. I turned tuna tartare into an ice cream cone and shrimp cocktail into a lollipop. Cotton candy left the circus and arrived in miniature on Park Avenue. In an increasingly super-sized world, I shrunk the ordinary, and in doing so made it fabulous, chic, and above all, delicious.

My business took off and became New York City's top catering company complete with a team of chefs, artists, and craftspeople to help me bring my imaginative ideas to life, everything served in one- or two-bite portions. Burgers, spaghetti and meatballs, BLTs, and even tacos instantly became

sophisticated when miniaturized and presented with style on a made-to-order tiered acrylic tray, under a hand-blown glass dome, or balanced on top of an entire lime or tomato. Screen stars, rock stars, sports stars, fashion designers, and even princes and princesses booked us to cater their milestone events. The idea of a Peter Callahan–catered party appealed to some of my biggest fans, like Martha Stewart, Kate Spade, and Joy and Regis Philbin.

My mother made everything from scratch when I was a kid, and I helped her out. (I even created my own sourdough culture.) Though I enjoyed cooking and baking, I never considered it as a career. I grew up in a town where everyone, including my father, went to work on Wall Street. So I did too. I worked for a commodities kingpin, and while it promised a prosperous future and I was doing well, working on the Street wasn't me. When I gave my notice, my boss said, "No one leaves here. You can't be that stupid!"

So in the mid-1980s, at the height of a bull run, I turned my back on Wall Street and got talked into taking on the lease of a small café out in the country. I sold my used Volkswagen Rabbit to buy a stove and opened for business without knowing a thing about professional food service.

Soon enough, it became clear that this was the stupidest thing I had done. But I couldn't turn back—I was determined to make this new career into *something*.

Gradually, more and more customers requested catered dinners. Catering was more lucrative than selling sandwiches in the café, but more importantly, it was more *fun*. I could offer jazzier foods and nicer presentations. Before I knew it my small-town café had turned into a successful New York City catering company. I was turning out parties with food like everyone else—which was a success in itself, but I wanted to do something more innovative. I made a decision that I would cater only *the best parties*. Fortunately my resolve to succeed kicked a reserve of untapped creativity into overdrive. It was my women clients on the Upper East Side who insisted that everything be served in one-bite sizes that made me start thinking about burgers and fries and spaghetti and meatballs in miniature portions. Prior to this, hors d'oeuvres had been so *serious*. I realized that mac and cheese canapés, or pig-shaped smoked salmon on black bread served in a field of wheatgrass, could add fun and humor to the cocktail hour while offering delicious food that everyone loves.

All of the hors d'oeuvres we serve are unique. It takes six months to a year to perfect an idea. Sometimes I work on an idea for years before I figure it out (chicken wings, for one, have eluded me for years!). The chefs on my team (eight to eighteen, depending on the season) and I collaborate on my vision to bring the concept to fruition. This is how we came up with interpretations in miniature of party classics from pheasant canapés under glass domes to potted shrimp served in edible pastry pots.

Whether it was a dinner in Tokyo or a celebration on a private island where everything has to be brought in by barge, people always talk about my food for years after a party, and many have asked me when I was going to write a cookbook so they could re-create their favorite party bites at home.

In this book, I've held nothing back. Most of the time, the recipe is exactly the same as the dish you'd get if you asked me to cater your party. Some of the time, I have incorporated shortcuts and made adjustments because the recipe is a little too labor-intensive to re-create at home (I have a battalion of chefs, prep cooks, and dishwashers, and I'm assuming you don't!). Often I include time-saving tips that make the creation of the dish simpler and quicker for home cooks. On that note, I strongly encourage you to read the Tips and Make Ahead sections of the recipes even before you read the cooking instructions, since they may change how you decide to approach the recipe. Being prepared is the key for pulling off a self-catered party like a pro.

Coming up with new ideas for party food is my favorite thing to do, and I am very grateful to have a job that is so creatively fulfilling. I hope this book provides you with inspiration for your own parties, be they casual family gatherings or a landmark occasion. Above all, have fun with your food!

kitchen tools + conveniences

PART OF WHAT MAKES the hors d'oeuvres in this book so special (aside from their deliciousness) is their presentation. Here is a list of items to help you get the look. Before beginning a recipe, make a list of the tools you will need and make sure you have them on hand. Preparation is the most important tool in your toolbox.

baking dishes
They're inexpensive and so functional. Have an assortment at the ready, including 8- and 9-inch square baking dishes, 9 × 11-inch baking dishes, and 9 × 13-inch ones.

baking sheets
Rimmed baking sheets measuring 11 × 18 inches (also called half-sheet pans) are a necessity. Quarter-sized sheets are useful, too.

blender
A good blender with a tight-fitting lid is a kitchen basic. It can purée anything from soup to frozen fruit for smoothies and cocktails.

blowtorch
A small handheld blowtorch is just the thing to brûlée the sugar on Oatmeal Crème Brûlée (page 169), the meringue on Baked Alaskas (page 185), and the marshmallow top for the Fluffernutters (page 194).

boxes
Silver cigarette boxes and small hinged wooden boxes are great for serving items like the Chicken Nori and Grape Leaf Cigarettes (pages 105 and 103) and the Foie Gras Truffles (page 109). You can fill the box with dried black beans and place the hors d'oeuvres on top so they have some height.

branding irons
One of my favorite ways to personalize a chicken breast (page 142). Or to spell out *BBQ!*

bricks
Want a perfectly flat strip of bacon? Weight it down under bricks as I do for the Corn Soup (page 76).

cast-iron skillet
You can do just about anything in a cast-iron skillet, but what it does the best is fry food. The cast iron heats evenly and keeps the oil hot and at a steady temperature. It's especially great for Fried Chicken (page 67). They're very inexpensive, too, so if you don't have one, there's no excuse not to get one.

cocktail shaker
For mixing margaritas and martinis in style.

cookie cutters
Start collecting biscuit or cookie cutters in lots of fun shapes and assorted sizes, from standard

round and square cutters to specialty dog-bone- and pig-shaped ones.

cups and glasses
Cordial glasses, mini tulip glasses, sake cups, silver mint julep cups, mini beer steins, espresso cups, and shot glasses are so versatile. Use them for drinks, cocktails, soups, and even for some desserts.

fine-mesh sieve
A medium to large fine-mesh sieve is great for straining the pecans for the Pecan Tarts (page 205), cabbage for the Vegetable Spring Rolls (page 127), and morels in the Stuffed Mushrooms (page 111). You can also use it as a pasta strainer instead of a colander.

food processor
A kitchen workhorse for finely chopping nuts and herbs or making pastes. Buying a model that comes with a smaller work bowl is a great idea—it comes in handy as a spice grinder or for processing small batches.

grill pan
I call for nonstick ridged and flat grill pans throughout the book. Ridged pans are great for getting that grill-marked look on Hot Dogs (page 45) and vegetables. A flat grill pan, or griddle, makes cooking Pancakes (page 162) and Grilled Cheese (page 53) a breeze.

instant-read digital thermometer
Indispensable for gauging the temperature of oil before frying or of meat before removing it from the oven. The kind with the probe attached to a base via a metal wire can be helpful—you can leave the probe in the meat in the oven or leave it in a pot of oil. They also have an alarm to let you know when the oil is too hot or when your meat is perfectly cooked.

knives
You don't need any special knives to make the dishes in this book, although keeping your knives sharp and honed will make the precision work easier. A chef's knife, paring knife, boning knife, serrated bread knife, and kitchen shears are the essentials.

loaf pans
For the Grilled Cheese (page 53) we use a 2¼ × 11¾-inch loaf pan, and for the Croque Monsieurs (page 138), which are a little larger, we use a 3¼ × 5¾-inch loaf pan (see Resources, page 250, for both sizes). While the latter is a standard-sized mini pan, the grilled cheese pan requires a special order. If you have the DIY gene, you can make your own by following the instructions on page 55. For the marshmallow layer of the S'mores (page 201), we use a regular 5 × 9-inch glass loaf pan.

lollipop sticks

Four-inch lollipop sticks are a must for the lollipops on pages 83 through 95. Small wooden or bamboo skewers can be substituted.

mandoline

For producing super-thin slices of plantain or potatoes for the cones on pages 96 and 99, a mandoline makes the job a cinch.

melon baller

Also called a Parisian scoop, this is a great tool for hollowing the tomatoes for Tomato Soup (page 53). You can also use it to make melon ball "ice cubes" for iced water or lemonade.

microplane grater

A can't-live-without tool for perfectly removing zest (and leaving the bitter pith behind) from citrus. Unlike a zester or a box grater, a Microplane grater removes zest in small bits, so after removing the zest, there's no need to chop it into smaller pieces.

mini muffin pan

With 24 muffin cups to a pan, mini muffin pans come in handy for making bacon cups for the Baked Beans (page 26).

mixing bowls

Amass as many as your cupboards can handle! Small mixing bowls, especially stylish ones, can double as serving dishes for nuts or other small finger foods.

pastry brush

A traditional pastry brush, a silicone brush, or even a small natural-bristle paintbrush from the hardware store is great for moistening edges of wontons when filling them, for brushing egg wash on pastry to give it a nice shine before it goes into the oven, or for brushing melted butter or olive oil onto vegetables before and after cooking.

pitchers and carafes

For cocktails, mixers, nonalcoholic beverages, and alcohol. Glass pitchers, vintage carafes, and decanters all work nicely.

platters and trays

How else are you going to serve your beautiful creations? Always keep an eye out for cake plates, tiered hors d'oeuvre stands, platters, and trays of all sizes. I like white platters with clean lines, but if your home is all about French Country, then choose colors and shapes that work with your décor

and taste. Mixing a few neutral-colored platters into the collection is a good idea.

popsicles
Mini popsicles call for mini popsicle sticks. I use $3 \times \frac{3}{8}$-inch popsicle sticks and a mini popsicle mold or two ice cube trays.

printer/scanner
A wonderful tool for customizing trays, coasters, and paper cones for Frites (page 42).

rolling pin
For rolling out dough or bread to make bread cups. A tapered French pin is lightweight, beautiful, and works like a charm.

ruler
A clear plastic ruler is easy to store and wash. A mini retractable tape measure is handy, too.

skillets
Nonstick and regular stainless steel skillets in all shapes and sizes.

slotted spoon and frying spider
These two utensils come in handy for cooking pasta, removing vegetables from a pot of broth, and turning Spicy Chicken "Fortune Cookies" (page 65) as they fry. A slotted spoon is simply a metal spoon that is perforated; it's infinitely handy. A frying spider is like a skimmer with a mesh net attached to it. It's one of those tools that you never realized you needed until you own it!

squeeze bottles
You put all that time and effort into making the food, so finish it with precision like a pro. Using a squeeze bottle to add a stripe of ketchup and mustard to a hot dog, or to place the perfect dot of crème fraîche on top of a blini, really finishes the look. They're inexpensive and useful, so buy a few.

stand mixer
A stand mixer makes mixing bread dough a snap. It's also convenient for cakes, cookies, and whipping egg whites and heavy cream. A hand mixer and a large bowl work for the latter, but for bread making, a stand mixer seals the deal.

steamer
A bamboo or metal steamer is required for making the Steamed Pork Buns (page 33). Bamboo steamers are definitely kitchen-to-table worthy, and they are very inexpensive, especially if purchased in a restaurant supply store.

tart pans
Baby 1- and 2-inch tart pans are so cute. They're essential for making the Mac and Cheese Canapés (page 25) and the cups for the Chicken Noodle Soup (page 41).

terra-cotta flowerpots
One-inch mini flowerpots are super-cute for serving the Potted Shrimp (page 122) if you decide not to make your own pastry pots.

tips and tubes
I use pastry tips for everything from piping chèvre for the Butternut Squash Lollipops (page 89) to frying potato cones to hold crabmeat (page 99). Cannoli tubes are perfect for frying mini taco shells—you'll need pairs of $\frac{1}{2}$-inch and 1-inch tubes (see page 72).

COMFORT FOODS

Peace of Pizza | Caprese Tea Sandwiches | Tuna Cheesesteaks

Mac and Cheese Canapés | Baked Beans in Bacon Cups

Sweet Onion Canapés with Mashed Peas | Twice-Baked Stuffed Potatoes

Steamed Pork Buns | Spaghetti and Meatballs

Vegetable Lasagnas | Chicken Noodle Soup

Cheeseburgers and Frites | Hot Dogs | Lobster Rolls

THE RECIPES IN THIS CHAPTER ENCOMPASS SOME OF the hors d'oeuvres I am most known for, like the bite-sized spaghetti and meatballs, as well as new creations like the Peace of Pizza. We make these tiny hors d'oeuvres with a consummate eye to detail. Cheeseburgers are served on home-baked mini poppy-seed buns with all the trimmings. Each spaghetti and meatball portion gets the perfect dot of marinara on top. What once would never in a million years be served at a fancy party, like French fries and hot dogs, have become some of my most-requested items at society events, and in turn, some of the most-requested items at parties across the country.

What makes these so popular is their small size and their universal appeal—because they taste just as delicious as their standard-sized versions. Comfort food connects people from all backgrounds and generations, making these hors d'oeuvres something that foodie culinary adventurers as well as meat-and-potato types can relate to. More than anything, they elicit big smiles when the tray comes out, because they're so unexpected.

peace of pizza

MAKES 2 DOZEN

Peace of Pizza is a retro-fabulous addition that is at once sophisticated and playful. If you can't find ready-made pizza dough, use mini pitas or halved English muffins as the base.

FOR THE PIZZA
1 14-ounce piece store-bought pizza dough
All-purpose flour, for rolling

FOR THE TOPPING
24 slices mozzarella cheese
½ cup store-bought marinara sauce

pizza | Preheat the oven to 450°F.

Place the pizza dough on a lightly floured work surface and roll it out ¹⁄₁₆-inch thick. Using a 1½-inch round cookie cutter, cut out 24 rounds of dough. Place the rounds on a rimmed baking sheet and prick each one with a fork. Bake until slightly golden, 2 to 4 minutes. Remove from the oven, set aside, and reduce the oven temperature to 350°F.

topping | Using a paring knife or a peace sign–shaped cookie cutter, cut each slice of cheese to form a peace sign. Spread 1 teaspoon of the marinara sauce over each pizza crust and top with a cheese peace sign. Return the baking sheet to the oven and bake just until the cheese is half melted, 1 to 2 minutes. (If you overcook the cheese, it will spread too much and won't look like a peace sign.)

serve | Using a spatula, transfer the pizzas to a platter. Serve hot.

MAKE AHEAD The baked pizza crusts can be stored in a gallon-sized resealable freezer bag in the freezer for up to 1 week. They can also be topped with sauce and cheese and refrigerated for several hours before being finished in the oven.

caprese tea sandwiches

MAKES 2 DOZEN

Caprese salad, that ubiquitous arrangement of fresh mozzarella, ripe tomatoes, and basil leaves, is the "it" dish for all the Hamptons "it" girls. Served in a mini pita, it makes a beautiful, fresh, and simple bite, which one client said "tastes like July." Baby heirloom tomatoes offer a sweet, juicy flavor that works well with extra-luscious buffalo mozzarella and good-quality extra-virgin olive oil.

12 2- to 3-inch mini pitas
2 ounces fresh salted mozzarella, cut into ¼-inch cubes
½ pint grape tomatoes or baby heirloom tomatoes, halved (about 1 cup)
¾ tablespoon extra-virgin olive oil
¼ teaspoon flaky sea salt, such as Maldon
½ cup fresh basil leaves, stacked, rolled, and thinly sliced crosswise into ribbons (or ½ cup small fresh basil leaves)
Freshly ground pepper

Divide the pitas in half so you have 24 half-moon pockets. Stuff each pocket with 3 to 4 pieces of mozzarella and set aside.

Place the tomatoes in a small bowl and drizzle with the olive oil. Add the salt and toss to combine.

Add some tomatoes to each pita pocket, and finish with a little basil and ground pepper. Serve immediately.

TIP Trader Joe's mini pitas work especially well. They're tasty and are the smallest we have found.

More Ideas for Mini Pitas | Mini pitas are a chic and simple solution to serving bite-sized sandwiches. Here are some other filling ideas:

- Lobster Salad (page 48)
- Baby spinach, feta, and Kalamata olives
- Cherry or grape-sized heirloom tomatoes, bacon, blue cheese
- Shredded rotisserie chicken, mayonnaise, grapes, and toasted walnuts
- Baby arugula, prosciutto, pesto, Parmigiano-Reggiano ribbons

tuna cheesesteaks

MAKES 3 DOZEN

I first experienced the cheesesteak sandwich when I went to boarding school in Connecticut. The highlight of my week was when we ventured into town for a sandwich at Apollo's Pizzeria. This tuna "cheesesteak" is an homage to Apollo's as well as to the classic Philly sandwich. The twist is that instead of using thinly shaved beef and melted cheese, I layer thinly shaved sushi-grade tuna, Pecorino cheese, and baby arugula on a homemade bun. If you don't have a mandoline to shave the Pecorino, a vegetable peeler will work great.

FOR THE TUNA
2 tablespoons soy sauce
1 tablespoon toasted sesame oil
1½ teaspoons honey
1 3-ounce, 3-inch-long block of fresh sushi-grade tuna, cut into 1-inch-thick slices
¼ teaspoon freshly ground black pepper
2 teaspoons vegetable oil

FOR THE VINAIGRETTE
1 large shallot
1 tablespoon plus ½ cup extra-virgin olive oil
Coarse salt
⅓ cup rice vinegar
2 tablespoons mirin (rice wine)
Grated zest and juice of 1 lemon
1½ teaspoons chopped fresh thyme leaves
Freshly ground black pepper

FOR SERVING
1 recipe mini Hot Dog Buns (page 45) or Quick "Homemade" Mini Buns (page 47)
8 ounces Pecorino Romano cheese, thinly shaved
2 cups baby arugula leaves

tuna | Whisk the soy sauce, sesame oil, and honey together in a small bowl. Submerge the tuna in the marinade and let it sit for 10 to 15 minutes.

Drain the tuna. Place the ground pepper on a small dish and sprinkle onto both sides of the tuna slices. Set aside.

Heat the vegetable oil in a medium skillet over high heat. Add a few pieces of tuna and quickly sear until just browned, about 10 seconds. Flip and sear the second side for another 10 seconds. Repeat with the remaining tuna. Let the tuna cool completely. Then stack the slices into a tower and place it on a long sheet of plastic wrap. Wrap tightly and freeze overnight.

vinaigrette | Preheat the oven to 350°F.

Place the peeled shallot in a small baking dish and toss with the 1 tablespoon olive oil and ¼ teaspoon coarse salt. Roast until the shallot is golden brown and soft, about 30 minutes. Remove from the oven, set aside to cool, and then roughly chop.

Place the rice vinegar, mirin, lemon zest and juice, thyme leaves, roasted shallot, and some salt and pepper in a blender and blend until roughly combined. While the blender is running, drizzle in the remaining ½ cup olive oil and continue to blend until smooth.

serve | Remove the tuna from the freezer. Let it stand at room temperature for 5 to 10 minutes (5 minutes if your kitchen is warm, 10 minutes if it's cool). Using a mandoline or a very sharp chef's knife, slice as thin as possible.

Use a serrated knife to slice a hot dog bun at a 45-degree angle, starting at the top right corner and slicing three-quarters of the way through the bun. Place 4 to 6 slices of tuna on the bun, followed by a few shavings of Pecorino and a few baby arugula leaves. Drizzle with the lemon vinaigrette, arrange on a platter, and serve.

MAKE AHEAD The vinaigrette can be made up to 2 days ahead; shake vigorously before using.

mac and cheese canapés

MAKES 2 DOZEN

I thought it would be fun to turn macaroni and cheese into an hors d'oeuvre, and party guests think these are witty. After *InStyle* magazine featured them, a rock star and his supermodel wife asked us to cater their Thanksgiving dinner! Cotswold cheese is a creamy cheese with chives added to it for punch—if you can't find it, you can substitute Double Gloucester or a subtle yellow cheddar.

FOR THE PARMESAN CUPS
Nonstick pan spray
1¼ cups finely grated Parmigiano-Reggiano cheese

FOR THE MACARONI
1 teaspoon coarse salt
1 cup elbow macaroni
2 cups heavy cream
1 cup grated extra-sharp white cheddar cheese
1 cup grated Cotswold cheese
1 cup grated Parmigiano-Reggiano cheese

24 edible flower leaves, for serving (optional; nasturtium leaves are pictured opposite)
¼ cup finely chopped fresh flat-leaf parsley

parmesan cups | Heat a medium nonstick skillet over medium heat. Lightly coat it with pan spray and then add 1 teaspoon of the grated Parmesan, using the back of the spoon to spread the cheese mound into the size of a silver dollar. Repeat twice so you have 3 cheese rounds cooking at once (if you have more than six 1-inch tart pans, you can cook more at once). Once the cheese is golden, after about 2 minutes, use a small spatula to carefully flip it over. Cook the other side until golden, 20 to 30 seconds, and then immediately transfer the rounds to 1-inch tart pans. Press a second tart pan on top of the first to mold the cheese rounds into the tart shape. Cool for a few minutes. Then lift off the top pan, remove the Parmesan cup, and set aside. Repeat making cheese cups until you have 24.

macaroni | Bring a large pot of water to a boil. Add the salt and the macaroni and return to a boil. Cook, following the package instructions, until the pasta is al dente. Drain and set aside.

While the macaroni is cooking, make the cheese sauce: Pour the cream into a large heavy-bottomed saucepan and simmer gently over medium to medium-low heat (be careful so the cream doesn't bubble up and out of the saucepan) until it is reduced by half, 20 to 30 minutes. Reduce the heat to low and add the cheddar, Cotswold, and Parmigiano-Reggiano cheeses; whisk until the sauce is completely smooth. Stir in the cooked macaroni and remove from the heat.

serve | If you are using them, arrange the nasturtium leaves on a platter. Portion 1 generous tablespoon of the macaroni and cheese into each Parmesan cup, sprinkle with parsley, place on the leaves, and serve.

MAKE AHEAD The Parmesan cups can be made up to 1 week in advance and stored in an airtight plastic container at room temperature.

The cheese sauce can be made up to 4 days before serving; cover and refrigerate. Rewarm it in a saucepan with 1 tablespoon heavy cream, whisking until smooth, and then stir in the cooked pasta.

> **TIP** Instead of making Parmesan cups, use a 1-inch round cookie cutter to stamp out rounds from sliced white bread. Sprinkle each round with some Parmesan and bake in a 350°F. oven until golden brown, 8 to 10 minutes.

baked beans in bacon cups

MAKES 2 DOZEN

We came up with this idea when we were hired to cater a party for a fashion company that was launching a new line of jeans. The inspiration was cowboys and pots of beans warming over a campfire. For parties, we fry the bacon cups one at a time so they get perfectly crisp and irresistible; for a less time-consuming preparation at home, I suggest baking them. Save the leftover habanero honey to add a sweet kick to barbecue sauce or to glaze grilled or roasted pineapple as a sweet side to grilled fish or chicken.

FOR THE HONEY
1 cup honey
1 fresh habanero chile, thinly sliced

FOR THE BEANS
1 tablespoon extra-virgin olive oil
1 large yellow onion, very finely chopped
2½ cups canned navy beans, drained and rinsed
¾ cup (packed) light brown sugar
2 thick-cut bacon strips, finely chopped
¼ cup port wine
3 tablespoons finely chopped fresh cilantro leaves
1½ tablespoons dark molasses
1 teaspoon chili powder
2 teaspoons coarse salt

FOR THE BACON CUPS
Nonstick pan spray
2 pounds thin-cut bacon

FOR SERVING
¼ cup sour cream
¼ cup finely chopped red or yellow bell pepper (or a combination of the two)
2 scallions, white and light green parts, thinly sliced

honey | Pour the honey into a small saucepan and bring to a simmer over medium heat. Turn off the heat, add the habanero, and allow the honey to cool to room temperature. Strain through a fine-mesh sieve into an airtight container.

beans | Heat the olive oil in a medium pot over medium heat. Add the onion and cook until translucent, about 3 minutes. Add the beans, brown sugar, bacon, port, cilantro, molasses, 1 tablespoon of the habanero honey, and the chili powder and salt. Stir to combine, and bring to a simmer over medium heat. Reduce the heat to medium-low and simmer gently until the mixture is reduced by half, about 20 minutes. Turn off the heat and set aside to cool to room temperature.

bacon cups | Preheat the oven to 350°F.

Turn a mini muffin pan upside-down and lightly coat the bottom with nonstick pan spray. Crisscross 3 slices of bacon over each upturned cup, and then place another mini muffin pan on top so that the bacon slices are compressed between the two pans. Place the pans on a rimmed baking sheet and bake until the bacon cups are crisp and browned, about 20 minutes. Remove the baking sheet from the oven and set aside to cool completely.

Lift off the top pan. Carefully remove the bacon cups from the bottom pan and place them on a paper-towel-lined baking sheet to drain, wrong side up.

serve | Gently reheat the beans in a saucepan over medium heat until warmed through (add 1 tablespoon water if they're too thick or dry). Place a spoonful of the beans into each bacon cup. Top with a dot of sour cream, some bell peppers, and a scallion ring. Serve.

MAKE AHEAD Both the beans and the bacon cups can be made up to 3 days in advance. Refrigerate the beans in an airtight container, and store the bacon cups in an airtight container at room temperature. (Don't rewarm the bacon cups before serving—they'll go soft.)

sweet onion canapés with mashed peas

MAKES 2 DOZEN

I came up with the idea for this canapé after an incredibly bountiful Thanksgiving feast with my family. Why not create mini versions of Thanksgiving dinner instead of the customary overflowing table? Creamed onions and peas are a must on my holiday table, and I thought, wouldn't it be great to offer this delicious and comforting classic in a single-bite size? Martha Stewart loved these when we served them at her Sirius radio launch party.

FOR THE ONION CANAPÉS
24 red pearl onions, peeled and both ends trimmed
2 tablespoons extra-virgin olive oil
½ teaspoon coarse salt

FOR THE MASHED PEAS
1½ cups fresh or frozen peas
¾ teaspoon coarse salt
⅛ teaspoon freshly ground black pepper
1 tablespoon unsalted butter, melted

Pea tendrils for serving (optional)

onion canapés | Preheat the oven to 450°F.

In a medium bowl, toss the onions with the olive oil and salt. Turn them out onto a rimmed baking sheet and roast until they're soft and just starting to caramelize around the edges, 15 to 20 minutes. Set aside to cool. Reduce the oven temperature to 350°F.

mashed peas | Place the fresh or frozen peas in a small saucepan and cover with water. Stir in ½ teaspoon of the salt and the pepper, and bring to a boil over high heat. Cook until very soft, 6 to 8 minutes. Drain, and immediately transfer to the bowl of a food processor or a blender jar. Add the melted butter and the remaining ¼ teaspoon salt, and purée until smooth, about 1 minute.

serve | Spoon a little of the puréed peas on top of each onion. Return to the oven and bake until warmed, 2 to 3 minutes. Transfer to a platter, top with a pea tendril (if using), and serve.

MAKE AHEAD The onions can be roasted 1 day in advance. Cover with plastic wrap and keep them at room temperature.

The peas can be puréed and refrigerated in an airtight container up to 1 day before serving.

twice-baked stuffed potatoes

MAKES 2 DOZEN

The Chef's Garden in Huron, Ohio, is well known for growing some of the most beautiful micro greens and mini vegetables. I was inspired to make a stuffed baked potato after receiving a package of their super tiny potatoes. The potatoes are so delicious as is, and we only enhance their tastiness by embellishing them with good butter and Stilton cheese.

12 garlic cloves, unpeeled
2 tablespoons extra-virgin olive oil
1½ teaspoons coarse salt
36 small potatoes, such as fingerlings or baby new
    potatoes
2 tablespoons unsalted butter, melted
½ teaspoon whole fresh thyme leaves
4 ounces Stilton cheese, cut into 24 small pieces
Chopped fresh chives

Preheat the oven to 350°F.

In a small bowl, toss the garlic with the olive oil and a pinch of the salt. Place the garlic on a rimmed baking sheet and roast until the cloves are golden brown, about 25 minutes. Remove from the oven and set aside to cool. Then pop the garlic out of the cloves and finely chop it.

Place the potatoes in a roasting pan and roast until a paring knife easily slips into the center, about 35 minutes. Remove from the oven and let cool for 10 minutes.

Use a paring knife to make a small slit in the top of each potato. Gently squeeze both ends of the potato to open the slit and push the fluffy insides up and out. Use a small spoon (like a ¼-teaspoon measure) to scoop all of the potato meat out of the skin, and place the meat in a medium bowl. Place the best 24 skins on a rimmed baking sheet and set aside.

Mash the potatoes with a fork. Then add the garlic, butter, thyme, and remaining salt. Spoon the mixture back into the skins (it should form a small mound on top of the potato), and return the potatoes to the oven. Bake until they're warmed through, 5 to 6 minutes.

Transfer the potatoes to a serving platter, and top each with a piece of Stilton and some chives.

MAKE AHEAD The potatoes can be baked and assembled up to 1 day before serving. Store in the refrigerator, covered with plastic wrap. Before serving, let them sit out at room temperature for 1 hour and then reheat them in a 350°F. oven until they're warmed through, 6 to 8 minutes. Top with the Stilton and chives.

steamed pork buns

MAKES 2 DOZEN

This idea came from David Chang's Momofuku Noodle Bar in New York City. David is famous for all dishes pork-related, but his tender and incredibly flavorful steamed pork buns are my absolute favorite. Since the pork filling for the steamed buns is so wonderfully rich, it's great served in small portions like this. I have two chefs who have worked for me for years, and they're especially adept at miniaturizing dishes in no time—they discovered that the trick for successful mini buns is to make sure that the bun is not too doughy. Marinating the pork belly for 8 to 24 hours adds tons of flavor, too.

FOR THE PORK
2 pounds pork belly
2 teaspoons coarse salt
1 teaspoon freshly ground black pepper
1 cup soy sauce
⅔ cup dry sherry
¼ cup honey
2 garlic cloves, finely minced
2 teaspoons grated fresh peeled ginger

FOR THE BUN DOUGH
1 teaspoon active dry yeast
Pinch of sugar
1 tablespoon plus 1 teaspoon warm (110°F.) water
2 cups all-purpose flour, plus extra for kneading
⅓ cup hot water
⅓ cup warm milk
2 teaspoons solid vegetable shortening
⅓ teaspoon baking powder
1 teaspoon vegetable oil

FOR THE PORK BUNS
2 teaspoons cornstarch
2 tablespoons warm water
¼ cup hoisin sauce

pork | In a shallow 9 × 11-inch baking dish, season the pork belly with the salt and pepper. In a medium bowl, whisk the soy sauce, sherry, honey, garlic, and ginger together. Pour half of this mixture over the pork, and refrigerate the remaining mixture. Cover the pork with plastic wrap and refrigerate for at least 8 hours and up to 24 hours.

Take the pork out of the refrigerator and uncover it. Preheat the oven to 325°F.

Place the pork in the oven and cook for 1 hour, basting with half of the reserved marinade every 15 minutes.

Tent the pork loosely with aluminum foil, return it to the oven, and continue baking, basting every 15 minutes, until it pulls apart easily with a fork, about 1½ hours. Remove the roast from the oven, transfer it to a cutting board, cover, and set it aside for 15 minutes. Pour the pan juices from the baking dish into a medium saucepan.

bun dough | While the pork is roasting, make the bun dough: In a small bowl, whisk together the yeast, sugar, and warm water until the yeast is dissolved. Cover with plastic wrap and set aside until it's foamy, about 5 minutes.

In a medium bowl, rapidly stir 1½ cups of the flour and the hot water together. Then stir in the yeast mixture, warm milk, shortening, and baking powder. Slowly sprinkle in the remaining ½ cup flour, stirring constantly until you have a soft dough. Turn the dough out onto a floured work surface and knead until it is soft and pliable, 2 to 3 minutes. Grease a large bowl with the oil, place the dough in the bowl, and turn it over to coat it with oil. Cover with plastic wrap and set aside until it doubles in size, about 1 hour.

(recipe continues)

Punch down the dough to deflate it, and turn it out onto a floured work surface. Divide the dough into 8 equal pieces and roll each into a ½-inch-thick log. Slice the logs crosswise into 1-ounce pieces, roll each into a ball, and place them on a lightly greased rimmed baking sheet. Cover with plastic wrap and set aside for 30 minutes.

pork buns | In a small bowl, mix the cornstarch with the warm water until it is completely dissolved. Mix the remaining marinade into the pan drippings in the saucepan. Add the cornstarch slurry and whisk together. Bring the liquid to a simmer over medium-high heat and cook, stirring often, until it is thick, 3 to 4 minutes.

Chop the pork into ¼-inch pieces and place them in a medium bowl. Add 4 to 5 tablespoons of the sauce, stirring well to make sure the pork gets evenly coated.

Use the palm of your hand to press each dough ball into a flat round. Place 1 teaspoon of the pork onto the center of each round, and wrap the dough up and around the pork. Pinch and twist the seam together to seal. Place the buns, seam side down, on a lightly greased rimmed baking sheet. Set the buns aside for 30 minutes.

serve | Line a stacked bamboo or metal steamer (a colander-steamer insert set into a pot works in a pinch too) with parchment paper. Place the steamer over simmering water and add some buns to the steamer, placing them 1 inch apart. Cover and cook until the dough is light and fluffy, about 4 minutes. Remove from the steamer and transfer to a platter. Repeat with the remaining buns. Serve warm, topped with a dot of hoisin sauce.

MAKE AHEAD The buns can be prepared, steamed, and then frozen for up to 3 weeks. Thaw the buns at room temperature and then re-steam them for 1 minute before topping with hoisin and serving.

DIY Pork Bun Station | Creating a make-your-own-pork-bun station for a casual party is less labor-intensive than stuffing them yourself, and most guests love interacting with food and lending a helping hand. Have bamboo steamers on the table, one filled with the steamed buns (you can buy regular size steamed buns at your local Asian market), and have the crispy pork in a different steamer lined with whole leaf lettuce. Some markets even sell ready-made crispy shredded pork that takes one less step out of the party planning equation.

spaghetti and meatballs

MAKES 2 DOZEN

One of my favorite restaurants in New York is the haute Chinese spot Mr. Chow, where I was once served traditional spaghetti and meatballs. I was so taken by the classic dish in the untraditional setting that it inspired me to turn spaghetti and meatballs into an hors d'oeuvre. Whether served at a posh wedding or for a kid's birthday party, this unexpected bite always creates a great buzz when it is paraded from the kitchen.

FOR THE PASTA SAUCE
1 2-inch piece carrot, finely chopped
1 2-inch piece celery, finely chopped
2 teaspoons chopped shallot (about ½ medium shallot)
1 bay leaf
1 garlic clove, thinly sliced
1 ½-inch piece cinnamon stick
1 cup heavy cream
2 teaspoons unsalted butter
2 teaspoons all-purpose flour
Coarse salt and freshly ground black pepper

FOR THE MEATBALLS
2 teaspoons extra-virgin olive oil
1 small shallot, finely minced
4 garlic cloves, finely minced
1 large egg, lightly beaten
2 tablespoons heavy cream
2 tablespoons freshly grated Parmigiano-Reggiano cheese
4 teaspoons tomato paste
2 teaspoons port wine
1 teaspoon coarse salt
Freshly ground black pepper
1 pound 90% lean ground beef
¼ cup canned or homemade beef broth

FOR SERVING
1 teaspoon coarse salt
8 ounces angel hair pasta
1½ cups store-bought marinara sauce, puréed in a blender
Freshly grated Parmigiano-Reggiano cheese
2 tablespoons finely chopped fresh flat-leaf parsley

pasta sauce | Place the carrot, celery, shallot, bay leaf, garlic, and cinnamon stick in a small saucepan and cover with the cream. Bring to a simmer over medium heat. Reduce the heat to medium-low and simmer until reduced by one third, about 20 minutes. Strain the sauce through a fine-mesh sieve (discard the solids) into a medium bowl, and then pour it back into the saucepan. Set it over low heat.

Melt the butter in another small saucepan over medium heat. Whisk in the flour and cook, stirring constantly, until the paste is straw-colored, about 30 seconds. Whisk in the reduced pasta sauce in a slow, steady stream until all of it is added. Once a few bubbles burst at the surface, season with salt and pepper and remove from the heat.

meatballs | Preheat the oven to 350°F.

Heat the olive oil in a medium nonstick skillet over medium heat. Add the shallot and cook, stirring often, until it becomes translucent, 3 to 4 minutes. Stir in the garlic and cook until fragrant, about 30 seconds. Turn off the heat and scrape the mixture into a large bowl to cool.

Once the shallot mixture is cool, whisk in the egg, heavy cream, Parmesan cheese, tomato paste, port, salt, and pepper to taste. Add the ground beef and mix gently with your hands until well combined. Shape the mixture into 1 tablespoon-sized balls and place them in a 9 × 11-inch baking dish.

Pour the beef broth into the baking dish, cover with aluminum foil, and bake until the meatballs are cooked through, 7 to 10 minutes. Remove the dish from the oven, discard the foil, and let the meatballs cool to room temperature. Slice a small bit off the top and the bottom of each meatball to create a flat surface; then place the meatballs on a serving platter.

(recipe continues)

serve | Bring a large pot of water to a boil. Add the 1 teaspoon salt and the pasta. Cook, following the package instructions, until the pasta is al dente, and then drain.

Reheat the pasta sauce over medium-low heat until warm. Stick a fork into the pile of pasta and twirl to make a 3- or 4-strand nest. Dip the nest into the warm pasta sauce and then carefully slide it off the fork and on top of a meatball. Repeat for the remaining meatballs. Finish each one with a dollop of the puréed marinara sauce, some Parmesan, and chopped parsley. Transfer to a platter and serve.

MAKE AHEAD The pasta sauce can be made up to 1 day ahead.

The uncooked meatballs can be frozen for up to 3 months. Let them sit out at room temperature for about 1 hour and then cook as directed.

The pasta can be cooked, twisted, and dipped in the sauce and then placed on the cooked meatballs up to 1 day ahead. Warm in a hot oven and then finish with the marinara sauce as instructed.

> **TIP** You can use a store-bought Alfredo-style pasta sauce instead of making your own.

VARIATION

mini meatball plates

Instead of making individual meatball bites, make small meatball plates. Simply divide the pasta between small plates (I like alternating red and white square plates for a riff on the red-checkered tablecloth effect), top with some marinara sauce and a meatball, and finish with chopped fresh parsley.

vegetable lasagnas

MAKES 2 DOZEN

Lasagna is such an Italian-American icon that I jumped at the opportunity to shrink it down to a cocktail-friendly serving. Riccia is a ribbon pasta similar to lasagnette (it is sometimes referred to as *mafaldine*; see Resources, page 250).

FOR THE PESTO
1 cup store-bought pesto
½ cup ricotta cheese
Coarse salt and freshly ground black pepper

FOR THE LASAGNA CHIPS
Coarse salt
2 2-inch-wide ruffled lasagna noodles
6 cups peanut oil

FOR THE LASAGNA
6 shallots
3 tablespoons extra-virgin olive oil
Coarse salt
12 ounces riccia or lasagnette pasta
12 ounces portobello mushrooms
¼ teaspoon freshly ground black pepper
1 cup jarred roasted red peppers, drained and sliced
    into 1 x ½-inch strips
1 4-ounce ball fresh salted mozzarella, cut into
    ¼-inch cubes
24 small fresh basil leaves

pesto | Place the pesto in a medium bowl. Stir in the ricotta. Taste, and season with salt and pepper if necessary. Set aside.

lasagna chips | Bring a large pot of water to a boil. Add 1 teaspoon salt and the noodles, and cook according to the package instructions until they're al dente. Drain, and place the noodles on a cutting board.

Divide each noodle into 3 lengthwise strips, and then slice the strips crosswise at 1½-inch intervals.

In a large pot, heat the oil to 350°F. over medium heat. Fry the noodles, in batches, until they're light brown and crisp, about 2 minutes. Remove the noodles from the oil with a slotted spoon or frying spider, and transfer them to a paper-towel-lined baking sheet to drain. Sprinkle with salt while they're still hot, and set aside.

lasagna | Preheat the oven to 350°F.

Place the shallots in an 8-inch baking dish and toss with 2 tablespoons of the olive oil and ½ teaspoon salt. Roast until the shallots are golden brown, about 30 minutes. Remove from the oven and set aside to cool. Once cool, purée them in a food processor, scrape into a small bowl, and set aside.

Bring a large pot of water to a boil. Add 1 teaspoon salt and the riccia pasta, and cook according to the package instructions until al dente. Drain, and place the pasta on your cutting board. Slice the pasta crosswise into 1-inch lengths and place them on a parchment-paper-lined baking sheet. Set aside.

Remove the stems and scrape out the gills from the mushrooms. Slice each mushroom in half horizontally, so you have 2 thin rounds of mushroom from each cap. Cut the rounds into ⅛-inch-wide strips and then crosswise into 3-inch lengths. Place the mushrooms in a medium bowl and season with the remaining 1 tablespoon olive oil, ½ teaspoon salt, and the pepper. Heat a grill pan over high heat and grill the mushrooms until both sides are grill-marked, about 30 seconds per side. Set aside to cool.

Place the baking sheet with the riccia pasta on your work surface. Top each length of pasta with a tiny bit of ricotta pesto, followed by a mushroom strip, a piece of roasted pepper, and a little more pesto. Cover with a mozzarella cube and then finish with ¼ teaspoon of the caramelized shallot.

serve | Preheat the oven to 350°F.

Place the fried lasagna chips on a parchment-paper-lined rimmed baking sheet and set a lasagna stack on top of each chip. Cover the baking sheet with aluminum foil and bake until the mini lasagnas are warm and the cheese is just starting to melt, 4 to 5 minutes. Transfer to a serving tray, finish each with a small basil leaf, and serve warm.

MAKE AHEAD The mozzarella and roasted peppers can be cut up to 1 day in advance.

The mushrooms can be grilled up to 1 day ahead, and the caramelized shallots can be prepared and stored in an airtight container in the refrigerator for up to 3 days in advance.

TIP Save time by forgoing the noodle bowl and instead serve the soup in Asian ceramic soup-spoons (see Resources, page 250).

chicken noodle soup

MAKES 2 DOZEN

In my take on chicken noodle soup, I turn an uncut sheet of fresh pasta into small soup bowls and fill each with chicken broth, vegetables, and shredded chicken. Adding a bit of miso (my wife's idea) gives canned broth a wonderfully savory depth of flavor.

FOR THE BROTH
1 14.5-ounce can low-sodium chicken broth
½ sweet onion, such as Maui or Vidalia, finely diced
1 fresh rosemary sprig
5 whole black peppercorns
½ bay leaf
1 celery stalk, finely diced
1 carrot, finely diced
2 tablespoons miso paste

FOR THE BOWLS
Nonstick pan spray
1 5 x 10-inch sheet of fresh pasta, cut into
   24 1½-inch squares

FOR SERVING
½ teaspoon table salt
2 ounces fresh angel hair pasta, sliced into 2-inch
   lengths
1 cup shredded cooked chicken (the meat from one
   fourth of a rotisserie or roasted chicken)

broth | Pour the chicken broth into a medium pot and add the onion, rosemary, peppercorns, and bay leaf. Cover and bring to a boil. Remove the lid, reduce the heat to a gentle simmer, and cook for 30 minutes. Turn off the heat, and strain the broth through a fine-mesh sieve into a clean pot; discard the solids. Add the celery and carrots to the broth and simmer over medium heat until they're tender, 8 to 12 minutes. Remove from the heat, and use a slotted spoon to transfer the vegetables to a small bowl; set aside.

Pour off all but 1 cup of the broth (refrigerate or freeze the remaining broth for another time) and bring it back to a simmer over medium heat.

Whisk in the miso, reduce the heat to medium-low, and simmer gently for 10 minutes. Set aside.

bowls | Preheat the oven to 325°F.

Lightly coat the insides of four 2-inch tartlet pans with pan spray, and press 4 pasta squares into them. Lightly coat the outside of 4 additional tartlet pans with pan spray, and fit them into the pasta-lined tart pans. Place the tart pans on a rimmed baking sheet and bake until the pasta is lightly browned and crisp, about 10 minutes. Remove from the oven. Once the pans are cool enough to handle, lift off the top tart pans and remove the pasta bowls. Spray the pans again if needed, and repeat with the remaining pasta squares to make a total of 24 bowls.

serve | Pour a ladleful of chicken-miso broth into a medium bowl and set aside. Bring a large pot of water to a boil. Add the salt and the angel hair pasta to the boiling water and cook until the pasta is al dente. Drain, and transfer to the bowl of broth to keep the noodles from sticking.

Reheat the chicken-miso broth over medium heat. Place the pasta bowls on a rimmed baking sheet. Add ½ teaspoon angel hair pasta, followed by 3 or 4 pieces of carrot, celery, and onion, to each bowl. Top with ½ teaspoon shredded chicken. Cover the baking sheet with aluminum foil and warm in the oven for 3 to 4 minutes. Remove the baking sheet from the oven and carefully ladle a little of the broth into each cup. Serve immediately.

MAKE AHEAD The baked pasta bowls can be stored in an airtight plastic container in the refrigerator for up to 1 week.

The chicken-miso broth can be refrigerated in an airtight container for up to 2 days.

cheeseburgers and frites

MAKES 3 DOZEN

This is my hands-down signature hors d'oeuvre. I've served it at Rockefeller weddings, rock star parties (like Tom Petty's book party), and celebrity birthdays (Kelly Ripa's son's party). Paired with our exceptionally crisp twice-fried frites, what makes our burgers better than others is their flavor. We serve the duo in customized tiered trays that have holes for the frites cones—for chic at-home parties, serve each frites cone in a shot glass so it stands upright.

FOR THE BUNS
1 recipe Bun Dough (page 45), prepared through
    the first rise
Flour
1 large egg
2 teaspoons poppy seeds

FOR THE FRITES
5 large Yukon Gold potatoes
6 cups peanut oil

FOR THE BURGERS
1 pound 90% lean ground beef
3 tablespoons Worcestershire sauce
½ teaspoon coarse salt
¼ teaspoon freshly ground black pepper
1 tablespoon extra-virgin olive oil
3 ⅛-inch-thick slices cheddar cheese, cut into
    1-inch squares

FOR SERVING
Coarse salt
Ketchup
12 cherry tomatoes, each sliced crosswise into thirds
3 to 5 large lettuce leaves, cut into 1-inch squares

buns | Punch the dough down, divide it in half, and place the halves on a floured work surface. Roll each piece of dough into a 20-inch-long log, and then divide the log into hazelnut-sized pieces. Roll each piece into a ball and place them on a parchment-paper-lined baking sheet, leaving about 1 inch between balls. Set the baking sheet aside and let the dough rise in a warm, draft-free spot until it feels airy and hasn't quite doubled in size, about 30 minutes.

Preheat the oven to 350°F.

In a small bowl, whisk the egg with 2 tablespoons water. Use a pastry brush to lightly dab the top of each dough ball with egg wash. Sprinkle each ball with some poppy seeds. Bake until the buns are golden brown, 8 to 10 minutes, rotating the baking sheet midway through. Remove from the oven and set aside to cool completely.

frites | Wash the potatoes and trim the ends so that each potato is 4 inches long. Slice a thin lengthwise plank off one side of each potato so you have a flat side. Starting with the flat side, slice the potato on a mandoline into ³⁄₁₆-inch-thick planks. Stack the planks and slice them lengthwise into ³⁄₁₆-inch-thick sticks. Place the potato sticks in a large bowl of water and set aside.

In a large pot, heat the oil to 350°F. over medium heat. Drain the potatoes and turn them out onto a paper-towel-lined baking sheet to dry. Then fry the potatoes in batches (so as not to cool the oil) until light golden brown but not cooked all the way through, 45 seconds to 1 minute. Use a frying spider or slotted spoon to transfer the fries to a paper-towel-lined baking sheet to drain. Be sure to reheat the oil between batches. Once all of the potatoes are fried and cooled, remove the paper towel and place the potatoes in the freezer until completely frozen, about 4 hours. Save the oil for the second fry.

Cut out thirty-six 4-inch squares of parchment paper and set them aside.

(recipe continues)

burgers (cook them in two batches, adding extra olive oil if needed) until they're browned on each side, about 1 minute. Place the burgers on a clean baking sheet and top each one with a cheese slice. Place them under the broiler until the cheese is melted, 1 to 2 minutes (check the burgers often as broiler intensities vary).

serve | Remove the fries from the freezer and re-fry them in batches until golden, about 1 minute per batch. Drain on paper towels and season with salt while hot. Fold each square of parchment into a cone shape and tape the seam to seal it.

Halve the buns and squeeze a small dollop of ketchup onto each half. Place a burger on each bottom bun. Cover with a cherry tomato slice, a lettuce square, and the top bun. Divide the fries among the paper cones and serve with the burgers.

MAKE AHEAD The baked buns can be frozen for up to 1 month in a resealable freezer bag. Let them defrost at room temperature for up to a couple of hours before using.

The uncooked burger patties can be frozen for up to 2 weeks. The burgers can go straight from the freezer into a hot pan—they'll take about 1 minute on each side to cook.

The once-fried and frozen fries can be kept frozen for up to 1 month.

> TIPS Skip making your own burger buns and use a 1½-inch round cookie cutter to stamp out mini buns from ready-made ones.
>
> Frozen fries can be fried in a flash instead of making your own.

Reheat the oil over medium heat until it reaches 350°F. Place an oven rack about 6 inches from the broiler element and heat the broiler to high.

burgers | While the oil is heating, make the burgers: Mix the ground beef with the Worcestershire sauce, salt, and pepper. Roll the mixture into 1-tablespoon-sized balls and place them about 1 inch apart on a rimmed baking sheet. Press each ball flat so it spreads into a 1½-inch wide, ½-inch thick patty.

Heat a large skillet (preferably cast iron) over medium-high heat. Add the olive oil and cook the

hot dogs

MAKES 3 DOZEN

My good friend Darcy Miller, the founding editor of *Martha Stewart Weddings,* asked me to shrink the hot dog, and then lots of other caterers followed suit. My favorite story is about one caterer who repeatedly sent a client hot dogs that were much bigger than ours. Again and again the client kept saying, "No, smaller, like Peter's," until the chef finally said, "You want small, I'll give you small," and broke the hot dog in half and handed it to her!

FOR THE BUNS
¾ cup warm (110°F.) water
1 teaspoon active dry yeast
1¾ teaspoons sugar
½ cup nonfat dry milk powder
2 large eggs
2 cups bread flour, plus extra for kneading
¾ teaspoon salt
4 tablespoons (½ stick) unsalted butter, at room temperature, cut into small pieces
1 teaspoon olive oil

FOR THE DOGS
2 teaspoons vegetable oil
36 mini cocktail franks

FOR SERVING
¼ cup mustard
¼ cup relish
¼ cup ketchup

buns | Whisk ¼ cup of the warm water, the yeast, and ¼ teaspoon of the sugar together in the bowl of a stand mixer. Cover with plastic wrap and set aside until foamy, about 5 minutes.

Uncover and pour in the remaining ½ cup warm water, the remaining 1½ teaspoons sugar, the powdered milk, 1 egg, and 1 cup of the bread flour. Sprinkle the salt over the flour and beat with the paddle attachment on low speed until the mixture is moistened, 1 to 2 minutes. Increase the speed to medium-high and beat the dough until smooth, about 10 minutes.

Stop the mixer and switch to the bread hook attachment. Add ¼ cup of the remaining bread flour and mix on low speed until most of the flour is absorbed. Add a few butter cubes and beat until they're incorporated. Then add another ¼ cup of flour. Continue to alternate adding flour and butter until they're both completely incorporated and the dough cleans the side of the bowl during mixing, about 7 minutes (add 2 to 3 more tablespoons flour if needed).

Knead the dough on a lightly floured work surface until it forms a ball, 2 to 3 minutes. Grease a large bowl with the olive oil, place the dough ball in the bowl, and turn it over to coat with oil. Cover with plastic wrap and set aside until the dough has doubled in size, about 1½ hours.

Punch down the dough, turn it out on a lightly floured work surface, and divide it in half. Roll each piece into a 12-inch-long, 1-inch-wide log. Cut each log into 18 small pieces. Roll each piece into an oval shape and then slightly flatten it. Place the pieces on a parchment-paper-lined baking sheet, leaving 2 inches between them. Cover with plastic wrap and let the dough rise in a warm, draft-free spot until the loaves are about ½-inch high, 12 to 15 minutes.

Meanwhile, preheat the oven to 350°F.

In a small bowl, whisk the remaining egg and 2 tablespoons water together to form an egg wash. Lightly dab the top of each dough ball with egg wash. Bake until the buns are golden brown, about 10 minutes, rotating the baking sheet midway through. Remove from the oven and set aside to cool completely.

(recipe continues)

dogs | Heat a ridged grill pan over high heat. Brush the grill pan with the oil and then place 12 franks on the pan. Cook until all sides have grill marks, about 2 minutes. Transfer to a parchment-paper-lined rimmed baking sheet and place in a 200°F. oven to keep warm. Repeat with the remaining franks.

serve | Place the mustard in a small squeeze bottle. Use a serrated knife to slice each bun at a 45-degree angle, starting at the top right corner and slicing three quarters of the way through the roll. Spread some relish on one side of the roll and ketchup on the other side. Place a grilled dog in the bun and stripe it with a squeeze of mustard. Serve immediately.

MAKE AHEAD The baked buns can be frozen for up to 1 month in a resealable freezer bag. Thaw them at room temperature for up to a couple of hours before using.

The franks can be grilled several hours ahead of time. Rewarm them in a 350°F. oven until hot, 3 to 4 minutes.

TIP If you don't have a squeeze bottle, make one by placing the mustard in a small resealable plastic bag and snipping ⅛ inch off one of the corners to make a small hole.

---

quick "homemade" mini buns

Instead of making your own hot dog buns, buy 3 containers of Pillsbury crescent dinner rolls. Carefully remove the dough from each can so it comes out as a rectangle and doesn't separate into the perforated triangles. There should be four 6 × 3-inch rectangles from each can (12 rectangles total). Slice each rectangle lengthwise into thirds, and then fold each third into thirds, so you have a 2 × 1-inch rectangle. Use a 1¾ × ½-inch oval cookie cutter to stamp out ovals from the folded dough. Bake at 350°F. for 10 minutes.

lobster rolls

MAKES 3 DOZEN

As a kid, I spent my summers at camp in Maine, sailing and lobstering, so it makes sense that I have a deep love for lobster rolls. This hors d'oeuvre shows up on almost every summer menu (and even some winter ones) that we put together.

FOR THE LOBSTER

1 cup dry white wine, such as Sauvignon Blanc
6 celery stalks, very finely chopped
6 medium carrots, very finely chopped
3 large yellow onions, very finely chopped
5 fresh cilantro sprigs (or basil, dill, or parsley sprigs)
1 1-inch piece fresh ginger, peeled and sliced into
    ¼-inch-thick rounds
¼ cup kosher salt
2 teaspoons whole black peppercorns
1 whole allspice berry
½ teaspoon whole cloves
1 ½-inch piece cinnamon stick
1 orange, quartered
½ lemon, halved
3 1-pound live lobsters

FOR THE FILLING

1 tablespoon mayonnaise
½ teaspoon truffle oil
Coarse salt and freshly ground black pepper

FOR SERVING

1 recipe Hot Dog Buns (page 45) or Quick "Homemade"
    Mini Buns (page 47)
36 fresh chervil leaves
36 lemon wedges

lobster | Place the wine, celery, carrots, onions, cilantro, ginger, salt, peppercorns, allspice, cloves, and cinnamon stick in a large stockpot. Squeeze in the juice from the orange and lemon wedges, and then add the juiced fruit rinds to the pot. Pour in 4 quarts water and bring to a boil. Reduce the heat to a simmer and cook for 1 hour. Turn off the heat and strain through a sieve into a large clean lobster pot or stockpot. Discard what remains in the sieve.

Bring the liquid back to a boil and add the lobsters. Quickly cover, reduce the heat to low, and cook for 8 minutes.

While the lobsters are cooking, fill a large bowl or tub (or your kitchen sink) with ice water and place it next to your stovetop.

Using tongs, remove the lobsters from the pot and plunge them into the ice water. Let the lobsters cool completely, about ten minutes.

Remove the lobsters from the ice water. Crack the shells and remove the meat (you should get about 12 ounces of lobster meat). Finely chop the lobster meat into ¼-inch pieces, place in a bowl, cover with plastic wrap, and refrigerate until serving (but no longer than 1 day).

filling | Whisk the mayonnaise and truffle oil together in a large bowl. Season with salt and pepper. Stir in the lobster meat and adjust the salt and pepper if necessary.

serve | Use a serrated knife to slice the rolls at a 45-degree angle, starting at the top right corner and slicing three-quarters of the way through the roll. Place a small amount of lobster filling in each roll, finish with a chervil leaf, and serve with a lemon wedge.

MAKE AHEAD The baked buns can be frozen for up to 1 month in a resealable freezer bag. Defrost them at room temperature for up to a couple of hours before using.

TIP Buy pre-steamed lobsters or lobster tails and use the meat to make the lobster rolls. The lobster meat will likely be tougher and less flavorful than if you boil them just before using, but it's the best way for those who don't want to boil a live lobster.

SHOTS + BITES

Tomato Soup and Grilled Cheese

Cheese and Wine | Caviar Spoons and Vodka

Buckwheat Blinis, Caviar, and Vodka | Fried Clams and Bloody Marys

Spicy Chicken "Fortune Cookies" and Cherry Sake

Fried Chicken and Coke | Beef and Beer

Fish Tacos and Gazpacho | Quesadillas and Margaritas

Corn Soup and Bacon | Beer and Pretzels

A TWO-SIP SHOT CLEVERLY MATCHED TO A SMALL BITE is an incredible icebreaker, especially when the small bite is playfully served on an edible spoon or inside a mini chinese take-out container. Having already shrunk my favorite foods, it was only natural to turn my attention to drinks, whittling them down to mini portions. Whether a simple shot of vodka to accompany caviar or a quick homemade cherry sake next to a chicken wonton "fortune cookie," my clients loved this idea because they had never seen anything like it. It wasn't long before I started thinking of "shots" in broader strokes—why not a green gazpacho for fish tacos or a shot of creamy tomato soup alongside a mini grilled cheese? Not only does the presentation add an element of surprise, it also gives people something to talk about.

tomato soup and grilled cheese

MAKES 3 DOZEN

This speaks to the kid in all of us, yet satisfies adult tastes with good-quality aged Gruyère and a home-made roasted-tomato soup. I like to rest the sandwich on the rim of the soup cup (the *New York Times* was so taken with this idea that they ran a feature on it). One of my trademarks is my home-baked bread made especially for mini sandwiches, burger buns, or rolls. If you don't have the time (or inclination), you can still pull off this fun bite: simply use sliced sandwich bread and a 2-inch square cookie cutter and *voilà*—instant minis.

FOR THE BREAD
Nonstick pan spray
12 ounces Bun Dough (page 45), prepared through the first rise
Flour

FOR THE SOUP
4 pounds ripe Roma tomatoes, halved lengthwise
1 large sweet onion, such as Maui or Vidalia, halved and each half sliced into quarters
8 garlic cloves, smashed
3 fresh basil sprigs
4 fresh thyme sprigs
½ cup extra-virgin olive oil
2 teaspoons table salt
½ teaspoon freshly ground black pepper
1½ tablespoons tomato paste
6 cups chicken broth, vegetable broth, or water

FOR THE SANDWICHES
8 slices aged Gruyère cheese
8 tablespoons (1 stick) unsalted butter, at room temperature

FOR SERVING
36 2- to 2½-inch vine-on red tomatoes

bread | Grease two 2¼ × 11¾-inch loaf pans (see Resources, page 250) with nonstick pan spray and set aside. (If you have only one mini loaf pan, prep half of the dough at a time, placing the other half in the refrigerator until you're ready to bake it. The chilled dough might need an extra 15 to 30 minutes at room temperature before baking, depending on the warmth of your kitchen.)

Punch down the dough to deflate it, and turn it out onto a floured surface. Divide the dough in half, shape each piece into an 11-inch-long log, and place them in the prepared loaf pans. Cover loosely with plastic wrap and set aside in a warm spot until the dough rises to the top of the loaf pans, 20 to 25 minutes.

Meanwhile, preheat the oven to 400°F.

Remove the plastic wrap, cover the pans with aluminum foil, and place the pans on a baking sheet. Bake in the oven until golden, 20 to 25 minutes. Remove the foil and let the bread continue to bake until it is golden brown, another 3 to 5 minutes. Take the bread out of the oven and set it aside to cool completely in the pans. Remove the cooled loaves from the pans, and use a serrated knife to cut each loaf into 36 thin slices.

soup | Preheat the oven to 350°F.

Place the tomatoes, onion, garlic, basil, and thyme in a 9 × 13-inch baking dish. Add the olive oil, sprinkle with the salt and pepper, and stir together. Roast until the skin starts to peel off the tomatoes and the onions begin to brown, about 30 minutes. Discard the basil and thyme sprigs, and transfer the vegetables to a large pot.

Stir in the tomato paste and the broth, and bring to a boil. Then reduce the heat and simmer gently, covered, for 20 minutes. Remove the pot from the heat, uncover it, and let the soup cool for 20 minutes.

Transfer about half of the soup to a blender (don't fill the blender jar more than two-thirds

(recipe continues)

full) and purée. Pour the purée through a fine-mesh sieve into a clean pot. Repeat with the remaining soup. Taste for seasoning and adjust if necessary.

sandwiches | Stack the cheese slices and slice the stack into 3 strips. Then slice them crosswise into thirds, creating 9 squares per slice. Butter one side of each bread slice. Place 2 slices of cheese on the unbuttered side of half of the bread slices and top with another bread slice, unbuttered side down, to make 36 sandwiches.

Heat a large nonstick griddle or skillet over medium-low heat. Cook the sandwiches in batches, browning each side until golden and crisp, about 1 minute per side. Serve immediately or allow the sandwiches to cool completely and follow the reheating instructions (see Make Ahead).

serve | Carefully slice the stem end off each tomato, removing about one fourth of the tomato; set these tops aside. Use a small melon baller to scoop the seeds and flesh out of each tomato, being careful not to puncture the wall of the tomato or make the wall too thin (it needs to be able to hold the soup without buckling).

Divide the warm tomato soup among the tomato cups. Place the tomato "lid" back on top and serve with the warm grilled cheese sandwiches.

MAKE AHEAD After buttering the bread and adding the cheese, the uncooked sandwiches can be individually wrapped in plastic wrap and frozen for up to 1 month.

Cooked and cooled sandwiches can be rewarmed on a baking sheet in a 350°F. oven until they are hot and the cheese is melted, about 3 minutes.

The soup can be refrigerated for up to 2 days, or frozen for up to 3 months.

DIY Bread Pan | Instead of purchasing small loaf pans to make the bread, you can make your own pans out of disposable aluminum ones.

Using kitchen shears, cut the sides and ends off a 12 × 8-inch disposable aluminum half-sheet cake pan so you're left with only the bottom rectangle. Cut the pan in half lengthwise so you have two 4 × 17-inch rectangles. Fold each of the two long sides up twice (to make a shallow U-shape) so the finished depth is about 1 inch. To close the ends, make 1-inch cuts along the crease where the side meets the end. Fold the center flap up and the side flaps in. Grease each pan with nonstick pan spray and proceed with the recipe.

cheese and wine

MAKES 3 DOZEN

A tongue-in-cheek ode to the classic pairing of cheese and wine, this hors d'oeuvre veers from tradition, offering the best of both in a clean, chic presentation. A thin wedge of pear is the foundation for a perfect sliver of Camembert that gets topped with a few edible flower petals and thyme leaves, adding a fresh, modern feel to otherwise typical party fare. I like to pour a crisp Chardonnay on the side (Bonterra makes a fabulous organic Chardonnay with pleasant apple and pear notes for less than $15 a bottle) to cut the Camembert's richness.

2 semi-ripe pears, preferably Bosc
1 lemon wedge
4 ounces cold Camembert cheese (see Tip)
2 fresh thyme sprigs
12 mini edible flowers, such as marigolds or violets
1 bottle crisp Chardonnay

Stand each pear on your cutting board, and using a paring knife, cut down around the core so you end up with 4 pieces of pear and a square-shaped core. Slice the pear wedges into ⅛-inch-thick pieces and squeeze a little lemon juice over them to delay browning. Place the slices on a paper towel to absorb the extra moisture.

Line a rimmed baking sheet with parchment paper. Slice the cheese into 36 1-inch-long, ¼-inch-thick triangles. Remove the rind if desired, and place them on the prepared baking sheet.

Arrange the pear slices on a tray or platter. Top each with a piece of Camembert, a few thyme leaves, and a flower petal. Pour the chilled wine into shot glasses (or cordial glasses, pictured opposite), and serve.

MAKE AHEAD The pears can be sliced up to 30 minutes before serving.

The Camembert can be sliced and refrigerated on a parchment-paper-lined rimmed baking sheet, covered with plastic wrap, up to 1 day in advance.

TIP For perfectly shaped slivers, freeze the Camembert for 1 hour before slicing. Let the sliced cheese sit out at room temperature for 10 to 20 minutes (depending on how hot the room is) before serving.

Shot Glass Alternatives | When it comes to serving a shot of wine, beer, or cola, there are many options. Sake cups, cordial glasses, mini tulip glasses, espresso cups, mini mugs, and of course shot glasses all work great. One of our favorite places to shop is Ikea—a great value for stylish, affordable, and modern stemware.

caviar spoons and vodka

MAKES 3 DOZEN

There are those who say that caviar should only be eaten from a mother-of-pearl spoon so as not to dilute its purity. That's a little too precious for me, so I came up with an edible spoon that pokes fun at the traditional way of serving caviar. This playful bite was one of the items we served at a party for Conan O'Brien in the *Saturday Night Live* studio after his last *Late Night* show.

FOR THE CRACKER SPOONS
¼ cup plus 1 tablespoon whole milk
3 tablespoons unsalted butter, cut into pieces
1 cup all-purpose flour, plus extra for rolling
1 teaspoon coarse salt
¼ cup grated Gruyère cheese

FOR SERVING
3 ounces American sturgeon caviar
2 tablespoons crème fraîche
Chilled vodka

cracker spoons | Chill the milk and the butter in the freezer for 10 minutes to get them very cold before making the crackers.

Place the flour and salt in the bowl of a food processor and pulse to combine. Add the chilled butter and pulse until the mixture resembles a coarse meal, with butter pieces no larger than a pea. Pulse in the cheese with a few short bursts, and then, with the processor running, add the milk and continue to process until the dough comes together into a very loose ball.

Transfer the dough to a large piece of plastic wrap and use the plastic wrap to press and form the dough into a ¼-inch-thick disk. Wrap the disk in the plastic wrap and chill for at least 1 hour or up to overnight.

Preheat the oven to 250°F.

Unwrap the chilled dough and place it on a lightly floured work surface. Roll the dough until it is 1/16-inch thick, reflouring the work surface and the top of the dough as needed. Stamp out spoons using a 4-inch-long spoon-shaped cookie cutter (the spoon part should measure less than 1 inch across). Use a thin metal spatula to slide under the spoons and transfer them to two parchment-paper-lined rimmed baking sheets. Gather the dough scraps, gently press them together, roll and stamp out the rest of the spoons, and place them on a baking sheet. Don't reuse dough scraps more than once.

Place the baking sheets in the oven and bake for 15 minutes (if you can't fit them side-by-side in your oven, then bake the spoons one sheet at a time). Remove the sheets from the oven and press the end of a wooden spoon lightly into the spoon part of the cracker to make an indentation. Return the sheets to the oven and bake until the spoons are very lightly golden and crisp, about 45 minutes, turning the baking sheets midway through baking. Remove from the oven and cool completely on the baking sheets.

serve | Arrange the spoons on a serving tray. Top each with a dollop of caviar and a drop of crème fraîche (use a squeeze bottle for a perfect drop). Pour the chilled vodka (1½ ounces / 3 tablespoons per person) into shot glasses, and serve.

MAKE AHEAD The spoons can be baked up to 1 week ahead. Store them in single layers separated by parchment paper in an airtight container at room temperature.

> **TIP** If you don't have time to make homemade spoons, stamp spoon shapes out of sliced white bread. Toast the bread spoons in a 350°F. oven until golden and dry, about 10 minutes. Cool before serving.

buckwheat blinis, caviar, and vodka

MAKES 2 DOZEN

Buckwheat blinis are a great addition or alternative to the edible spoons when serving caviar. You can serve them alongside vodka shots like the caviar spoons on page 59, or with small airport bottles of Stoli vodka, with a mini straw to complete the look.

FOR THE BLINIS
2 large eggs, separated
½ cup sour cream
½ teaspoon baking soda
½ cup all-purpose flour
¼ cup buckwheat flour
2 teaspoons sugar
½ teaspoon baking powder
Pinch of coarse salt
2 tablespoons unsalted butter, at room temperature
Melted unsalted butter, for cooking the blinis

FOR SERVING
2 ounces American sturgeon caviar
1 tablespoon crème fraîche
Chilled vodka

blinis | In a medium bowl, whisk the egg yolks. Add the sour cream and baking soda, and whisk to combine. Then, using a wooden spoon, stir in the all-purpose and buckwheat flours, sugar, baking powder, and salt until well combined. Stir in the room-temperature butter until thoroughly incorporated.

In the bowl of a stand mixer (or in a large bowl if using a hand mixer), beat the egg whites until stiff, shiny peaks form (when the whip is lifted from the whites, a tall, stiff peak should remain). Fold the egg whites into the batter until just a few white streaks remain.

Brush a large nonstick skillet (preferably one with sloped sides) or a flat nonstick griddle with some melted butter and place over medium heat. Add a small spoonful of batter (about 1 teaspoon of batter so the blini expands to about the size of a quarter). Repeat a few times, leaving enough space between blinis so they don't run together, and cook until the edges of the blinis are dry, 1 to 2 minutes. Then flip the blinis over and cook until the other sides are browned, 30 seconds to 1 minute. Use a spatula to transfer the blinis to a parchment-paper-lined baking sheet, and set aside. Cook the rest of the batter and let the blinis cool to room temperature.

serve | Place the blinis on a serving tray. Finish each with a dollop of caviar and a drop of crème fraîche (use a squeeze bottle for a perfect drop). Pour the chilled vodka (1½ ounces / 3 tablespoons per person) into shot glasses, and serve.

MAKE AHEAD To freeze the cooked blinis, place them in a single layer on a parchment-paper-lined baking sheet and freeze until semi-frozen, 1 to 2 hours. Then wrap each one in plastic wrap and transfer them to a gallon-sized freezer bag; freeze for up to 2 weeks. Let them sit at room temperature for 2 hours before serving.

fried clams and bloody marys

MAKES 2 DOZEN

Fried clams are one of my guilty pleasures. My wife and I always stop at a clam shack for a basket on our way to our Nantucket house, and those outings inspired this dish. The crispy fried clams are excellent with a jalapeño-flecked aioli and a boldly spiced Bloody Mary. Presentation is simple—just nestle them back into their shells for a stylish beach-y vibe.

FOR THE AIOLI
2 garlic cloves
1 teaspoon extra-virgin olive oil
Coarse salt
1 jalapeño pepper, halved, seeded, and deribbed
2 tablespoons fresh lemon juice
1 cup mayonnaise
3 to 4 drops hot sauce
Freshly ground black pepper

FOR THE BLOODY MARYS
2 cups tomato juice
1 tablespoon prepared horseradish
1 tablespoon fresh lemon juice
¾ teaspoon hot sauce
¼ teaspoon Worcestershire sauce
¼ teaspoon freshly ground black pepper
¾ cup chilled vodka
Celery leaves, for serving (optional)

FOR THE CLAMS
24 littleneck clams, shucked, shells reserved
Grated zest of 1 lemon
2 tablespoons finely chopped fresh flat-leaf parsley
1 cup buttermilk
1 cup panko breadcrumbs
2 tablespoons extra-virgin olive oil
4 cups peanut or vegetable oil
Flaky sea salt, such as Maldon, for sprinkling
1 jalapeño pepper, halved, seeded, deribbed, and sliced into small pieces

aioli | Preheat the oven to 350°F.

Place the garlic, olive oil, and a pinch of salt in the middle of a 3-inch square of aluminum foil. Fold the foil around the garlic to completely enclose. Roast until tender, about 20 minutes. Remove from the oven and set aside to cool.

Place the garlic, jalapeño, and lemon juice in a food processor (preferably a mini food processor) and process to a smooth paste. Turn off the machine and add the mayonnaise, hot sauce, and salt and pepper to taste; process to combine. Scrape into a bowl, cover directly with plastic wrap, and refrigerate.

bloody marys | In a large pitcher or measuring cup, whisk together the tomato juice, horseradish, lemon juice, hot sauce, Worcestershire, and pepper. Taste, and adjust the seasonings if needed. Pour in the vodka and refrigerate. (Reserve the celery leaves.)

clams | Place the clams in a medium bowl. Add the lemon zest and parsley and set aside to marinate for 10 minutes. Meanwhile, pour the buttermilk into a small bowl and place the breadcrumbs in a medium bowl. Drizzle the olive oil over the breadcrumbs and toss together with a fork until the breadcrumbs are evenly moistened.

Dunk the clams in the buttermilk, remove with a slotted spoon or fork, roll them around in the breadcrumbs until evenly coated, and then place them on a rimmed baking sheet.

In a medium pot, heat the peanut oil to 350°F. over medium heat.

Add about half of the clams and fry until they are golden brown and crisp, 1½ to 2 minutes. Remove the clams from the oil with a frying spider or slotted spoon, place them on a paper-towel-lined plate to drain, and season with sea salt. Repeat with the remaining clams.

serve | Place each fried clam in a reserved clamshell. Top each clam with a drop of jalapeño aioli and a piece of jalapeño, and stick a small wooden fork in it. Pour the Bloody Marys into shot glasses or small bottles, finish each with a celery leaf (if using), and serve with the clams.

MAKE AHEAD The aioli can be prepared up to 2 days in advance and refrigerated.

The Bloody Marys can be mixed up to 1 day ahead and refrigerated.

The breaded clams can be kept frozen for up to 1 month. Cook them, still frozen, for 2 to 2½ minutes in the hot oil.

TIPS To quickly chill a drink or wine, pour it into a cocktail shaker and add ice. Then strain out the liquid and divide it between shot glasses.

Save the leftover steaming liquid from the clams to make a seafood risotto.

peace, happiness and prosperity

spicy chicken "fortune cookies" and cherry sake

MAKES 2 DOZEN

Eleni Gianopulos, of Eleni's Cookies in New York City, asked me to come up with a new idea for her husband Randall's Chinese-themed dinner party, and I was very happy to have dreamt this up. These savory chicken wonton "fortune cookies" nestled into our homemade 1-inch Chinese take-out boxes were a huge hit (if using standard-sized take-out boxes, fill with three to four wontons). There is an enlightening process of discovery when the guests read the fortunes, written on small strips of paper (and often customized for the event). A cherry sake shot is a fun way to finish off the bite.

FOR THE SAKE
2½ cups sake
1 cup black cherry juice

FOR THE CHICKEN "FORTUNE COOKIES"
8 ounces boneless, skinless chicken breast, chopped into 1-inch cubes
1 scallion, white and light green parts only, finely chopped
1½ teaspoons hoisin sauce
½ teaspoon finely grated peeled fresh ginger
½ teaspoon your favorite hot sauce (we like Sriracha sauce)
½ teaspoon salt
½ teaspoon freshly ground black pepper
1 12-ounce package round or square wonton wrappers
1 small round potato
6 cups peanut oil
2½-inch long x ¼-inch wide paper strips with fortunes
Curly parsley (optional; to prop up wontons in the boxes)
Store-bought Chinese take-out boxes (see Resources, page 250)

sake | Stir the sake and juice together in a pitcher. Cover with plastic wrap and chill in the refrigerator.

chicken "fortune cookies" | Place the chicken, scallion, hoisin sauce, ginger, hot sauce, salt, and pepper in the bowl of a food processor and pulse until rough-textured and thoroughly combined.

Set a small bowl of water on the counter. Separate the wonton wrappers and lay them out on your work surface. Slice the lower third off the potato so it stands upright. Stick a paring knife halfway into the side of the potato so half of the blade is exposed (and so the sharp edge faces down). You'll use the dull spine of the blade to help shape the "fortune cookies."

Line a rimmed baking sheet with parchment paper and set it aside. Place 1 teaspoon of the chicken mixture in the center of each wonton wrapper. Dip a pastry brush or your finger into the bowl of water and wet the outer edge of the entire wrapper. Fold the top portion of the wrapper over to meet the bottom and press down along the edges to seal. Place the filled belly of the wonton on top of the spine of the knife blade and gently press the wonton down to make a fortune cookie shape (the knife/potato method makes a tight pocket in the wonton for tucking in the fortune later). Place the shaped wonton on the prepared baking sheet and repeat with the remaining wontons. Freeze the wontons for 30 minutes.

In a large saucepan, heat the oil to 350°F. over medium heat. Add a few wontons at a time (avoid overcrowding the pot; otherwise the temperature of the oil will drop and the wontons will be greasy) and fry until golden brown on all sides, 2 to 3 minutes. Transfer the cooked wontons to a paper-towel-lined baking sheet.

(recipe continues)

serve | While the wontons are still hot, insert a paper fortune into the crease so it sticks straight up (or place the fortune on top of the wonton). Place 1 wonton in each take-out box (if the boxes are on the larger side, you can fill them with a bed of curly parsley to prop up the wonton). Serve with chilled cherry sake on the side.

MAKE AHEAD The filled uncooked wontons can be frozen for up to 3 months.

The fried wontons can be cooled and held at room temperature for up to 2 hours before serving. To rewarm, place them on a rimmed baking sheet and heat in a 350°F. oven until hot, 3 to 4 minutes.

The cherry sake can be refrigerated for up to 1 week.

TIPS Instead of making your own wontons, buy frozen chicken gyoza-style potstickers at the grocery store and steam them according to the package instructions. Place them on a plate to cool slightly, and then fold each one around a chopstick so both ends meet. Skewer a toothpick through the ends to hold them in place, and remove the chopstick. Fry and serve according to the instructions above.

For alcohol-free options, replace the cherry sake with a shot of watermelon juice, cherry cola, or sparkling cider.

DIY Pupu Platter |

Who doesn't love the giant pupu appetizer platters served in Chinese restaurants? Creating your own take on it is a fun way to present several hors d'oeuvres at once. Instead of branding the BBQ Chicken, present them as lollipops with a mini hibachi grill so guests can grill their own. Here are some ideas to get you started:

- Chicken "Fortune Cookies"
- Spicy Beef "Fortune Cookies"
- BBQ Chicken (not branded) (page 142)
- Vegetable Spring Rolls (page 127)
- Chicken-Nori Rolls (page 105)
- Steamed Pork Buns (page 33)

fried chicken and coke

MAKES 2 DOZEN

I love using symbols of Americana for my hors d'oeuvres, and Coca-Cola is definitely an icon that reaches across generational divides and rises to a stature that is so much more than just a soda. My idea was to have mini bottles hand-blown by an artisan glass blower, but then, to our good fortune, we discovered these adorable ready-made ones. Coming up with a suitable partner to a Coke was a cinch: crisp and juicy fried chicken. Even those who don't typically indulge in this kind of decadent comfort food can't resist the temptation of the pair when served in small portions. If you can't find mini Coke bottles, you can serve the fried chicken cups alongside shots of Coke.

FOR THE SALSA
1¼ cups diced green tomato (about 1 large)
2 tablespoons diced, peeled cucumber
1 scallion, light green and white parts only, finely chopped
1 teaspoon minced jalapeño pepper (seeded if desired for less heat)
1 tablespoon fresh lime juice
2 tablespoons finely chopped fresh cilantro
Coarse salt and finely ground black pepper

FOR THE FRIED CHICKEN
1 cup buttermilk
1 garlic clove, finely minced
1 tablespoon your favorite hot sauce (we like Sriracha sauce)
1 teaspoon hot paprika
2 teaspoons cayenne pepper
6 ounces chicken tenders (or 1 boneless, skinless chicken breast sliced into 1-inch-wide strips)
2 cups peanut oil
1 cup all-purpose flour
1 teaspoon chili powder
2 teaspoons coarse salt
½ teaspoon freshly ground black pepper

FOR THE CUPS
4 chicken breasts, skin on
Coarse salt and freshly ground black pepper

FOR SERVING
24 mini bottles of Coke (or 4½ cups Coca-Cola)

salsa | Mix the green tomato, cucumber, scallion, jalapeño, lime juice, and cilantro in a large bowl. Season to taste with salt and pepper. Cover with plastic wrap and refrigerate overnight.

fried chicken | Pour the buttermilk into a gallon-sized resealable food storage bag. Add the garlic, hot sauce, paprika, and 1 teaspoon of the cayenne. Seal the bag shut and shake to combine. Add the chicken tenders to the bag, seal, and refrigerate overnight.

In a cast-iron or heavy-bottomed skillet, heat the oil to 350°F. over medium heat. Place the flour, the remaining 1 teaspoon cayenne, and the chili powder, salt, and pepper in a resealable gallon-sized bag. Seal, and shake to combine. Transfer about half of the seasoned flour to a second bag. Remove the chicken from the marinade, allowing the excess to drip off, and place it in one of the bags. Seal the bag and shake to coat the chicken. Return the chicken to the marinade and coat it evenly, and then transfer the chicken to the second bag of flour. Shake off any excess flour, and place the chicken in the hot oil. Cook until the chicken is golden, about 1½ minutes per side. Transfer to a paper-towel-lined plate, and then place the chicken on a cutting board and dice it into ¼-inch cubes.

(recipe continues)

cups | Preheat the oven to 375°F.

Gently pull the chicken skin off the breasts (refrigerate or freeze the breasts for another time) and lay it on a parchment-paper-lined rimmed baking sheet. Pull all sides of the skin to make it as flat as possible, and season with salt and pepper. Place another baking sheet on top of the skin and weight it down with a couple of bricks or a small pot filled with water. Bake the skin for 20 minutes. Remove the baking sheets from the oven (keep the oven on) and let the skin cool completely, with the top baking sheet on.

Place the chicken skin on a cutting board and use a 2-inch round cookie cutter to stamp out rounds. Place each round in the cup of a 24-cup mini muffin tin, and place a second mini muffin tin on top. Weight down the second tin with a few bricks or a small pot of water. Bake for 10 minutes. Remove from the oven and cool for 10 minutes, with the top baking sheet on, before removing the skins from the cups. They should be crispy.

serve | If using shots of cola, pour it into 24 shot glasses. Divide the fried chicken among the chicken skin cups. Top each one with a little salsa, and serve each fried chicken cup alongside a mini bottle or shot of Coke.

MAKE AHEAD The crispy chicken skin cups can be made the night before serving and stored in an airtight container at room temperature.

The salsa can be made 2 days ahead.

TIPS Instead of making the chicken skin cups, use thick-cut potato chips for serving.

Coca-Cola made with cane sugar has a far superior caramel flavor and more fizz than its corn-syrup-sweetened cousin. You can find cane-syrup Coke at some Latin markets (where it's imported from Mexico) or stock up on it during Passover, when Coke is made according to kosher dietary laws—with cane sugar.

If you want to add to the all-American character of this hors d'oeuvre, serve shots of rum and Coke: mix 3 cups of cola with 1 cup of dark rum.

beef and beer

MAKES 2 DOZEN

I created this as a nod to those meat-and-beer halls where the boys go after the big game, the kind of place where there's a giant slab of roast beef at a carving table. I refined the concept a bit, but at its core, it's still a very manly raw beef paired with thick, dark suds (albeit in a 2-inch mug).

FOR THE PARMESAN TOASTS
2 dense baguettes (you don't want an airy baguette with lots of holes in it)
½ cup finely grated Parmigiano-Reggiano cheese

FOR THE CARPACCIO
3-ounce, 6-inch-long piece of filet mignon, boneless rib steak, or boneless strip steak
Coarse salt and freshly ground black pepper
½ cup fresh parsley leaves, roughly chopped
¼ cup fresh tarragon leaves, roughly chopped
½ cup roughly chopped fresh chives
1 cup baby arugula leaves
½ teaspoon truffle oil (preferably white truffle oil)
Sea salt

FOR SERVING
3 bottles chilled Guinness beer (or other stout-style beer)

parmesan toasts | Preheat the oven to 375°F.

Place the baguettes on your work surface and slice away the crusts so you are left with 2 crustless rectangular baguettes. Evenly slice the baguettes lengthwise into 4 long pieces. Lay each piece down and use a 1-inch cookie cutter to punch out 24 rounds. Place the rounds on a parchment-paper-lined rimmed baking sheet. Sprinkle each round with 1 teaspoon of the Parmigiano-Reggiano cheese.

Bake the baguettes until the cheese is melted and golden brown, 10 to 12 minutes. Remove the baking sheet from the oven and let the Parmesan toasts cool completely before removing them from the pan.

carpaccio | Slice the steak lengthwise into ½-inch-thick planks, and season both sides with coarse salt and pepper. On a large plate and using your fingertips, mix the herbs together. Sprinkle the herbs as evenly as possible onto each side of the meat, patting them down so they stick.

Place a 12-inch-long piece of plastic wrap on your work surface. Lay the meat on top of the plastic, leaving a 2-inch space at the bottom. Starting at the bottom, use the plastic to push and roll the beef into a tight spiral (like rolling sushi; don't wrap the plastic into the spiral, just use it to help roll a tight cylinder of meat). Once you reach the end, twist the ends of the plastic wrap shut (like a Tootsie Roll) pushing out all the air so the package is airtight. Freeze for at least 4 hours.

Remove the rolled meat from the freezer and discard the plastic wrap. Slice the meat crosswise as paper-thin as possible. You should get about 25 slices. (If you happen to have a meat slicer, set it to the #2 setting; you'll get about 50 slices.)

Set the slices on a parchment-paper-lined baking sheet (if you have more than one layer, separate them with plastic wrap). Cover the entire baking sheet tightly with plastic wrap and freeze until ready to use.

serve | Stack about 12 baby arugula leaves, roll them into a tight cylinder, and thinly slice them crosswise into ribbons. Place the arugula in a medium bowl and repeat with the remaining leaves. Drizzle the truffle oil over the arugula, and sprinkle with a pinch of sea salt. Toss to coat and set aside.

Place the toasts on a serving tray. Remove the beef from the freezer. Lay 1 slice of beef on top of each toast (2 if sliced by machine). Arrange a small mound of arugula over the beef. Pour the beer into small mugs (or shot glasses), and serve alongside the toasts.

MAKE AHEAD The baked Parmesan toasts can be stored in an airtight container at room temperature for up to 1 week.

The beef carpaccio can be rolled and frozen for up to 2 weeks before serving, and can be sliced and frozen up to 2 days ahead.

TIP In place of the baguettes, use a loaf of sliced white sandwich bread. Use a 1-inch cookie cutter to stamp out the rounds from each slice, and make the Parmesan toasts as instructed.

fish tacos and gazpacho

MAKES 2 DOZEN

Fish tacos are transformed from casual taco truck fare to a sophisticated starter when they are loaded with citrus-marinated cod, a creamy avocado topping, spicy jalapeño, and sweet mangos. I've always thought that the best design is most often the simplest, and these tacos, in their stylish and vibrant lime holder, drive that point home. Refreshing gazpacho shooters made with lots of fresh herbs, green grapes, and cucumber provide a great balance to the sweet-spicy taco crunch.

FOR THE GAZPACHO
1 cup seedless green grapes
½ seedless (English) cucumber, peeled and chopped
½ green bell pepper, seeded, deribbed, and chopped
¼ jalapeño pepper, seeded, deribbed, and finely chopped
½ cup fresh cilantro leaves
¼ cup roughly chopped fresh chives
2 tablespoons extra-virgin olive oil
¼ cup fresh lime juice (from 4 to 5 limes)
Coarse salt and freshly ground black pepper

FOR THE TACO SHELLS
6 cups peanut oil
2 10-inch flour tortillas

FOR THE TACOS
1 tablespoon extra-virgin olive oil
¼ teaspoon grated lemon zest
¼ teaspoon grated lime zest
⅛ teaspoon coarse salt
Pinch of freshly ground black pepper
1 4- to 6-ounce fresh cod fillet

FOR SERVING
½ ripe avocado
½ teaspoon fresh lemon juice
Pinch of coarse salt
Freshly ground black pepper
24 limes
¼ jalapeño pepper, seeded, deribbed, and finely chopped
1 small ripe mango, seeded and diced into ¼-inch cubes

gazpacho | Place the grapes, cucumber, bell pepper, jalapeño, cilantro, chives, olive oil, and lime juice in the bowl of a food processor, or in a blender, and purée. Strain through a fine-mesh sieve into a pitcher, and stir in salt and pepper to taste. Cover with plastic wrap and refrigerate until serving.

taco shells | In a large pot, heat the oil to 325°F. over medium heat.

While the oil heats, prepare the tortilla shells: Place the tortillas on your work surface, and use a 2-inch round cookie cutter to stamp 12 rounds from each tortilla. Wrap a tortilla round around a ½-inch cannoli tube and then slide it inside a 1-inch tube. Repeat with 5 more tortilla rounds. Place the 6 tubes in the oil and cook until the tortillas look golden, about 1 minute. Remove the tubes from the oil and place them on a paper-towel-lined baking sheet to cool.

Once cool, carefully slide the fried shells and the ½-inch tubes out of the larger tubes. Remove the crisp shells and set them aside. Repeat with the remaining tortilla rounds.

tacos | In a small bowl, whisk together the oil, lemon and lime zest, salt, and pepper. Place the cod fillet in a baking dish or on a rimmed baking sheet (the baking dish or sheet pan should be long enough so the fillet rests flat) and rub with the marinade. Cover with plastic wrap and refrigerate for 30 minutes.

Meanwhile, preheat the oven to 450°F.

Remove the cod from the refrigerator, discard the plastic wrap, and roast it in the oven until the thickest part flakes apart easily when pierced with a fork, 6 to 8 minutes. Set aside to cool completely, and then flake the fish with your fingers or a fork.

serve | Scoop the avocado flesh out of the skin, place it in a small bowl, and mash with a fork. Stir in the lemon juice, salt, and some pepper, and set aside.

Slice a thin piece off one long side of each lime so it doesn't wobble. Rest the lime on the cut side. Using a paring knife, cut a ¼-inch-deep, 1-inch-wide V-shaped notch into the top of the lime (this will be the cradle for the taco).

Place ¼ teaspoon mashed avocado in each taco shell. Divide the flaked cod among the tacos, and sprinkle the jalapeño and mango on top. Set the tacos into the prepared lime holders. Divide the gazpacho among twenty-four small glasses, and serve one with each taco.

MAKE AHEAD The taco shells can be fried and stored in an airtight container at room temperature for up to 1 week.

The gazpacho can be made up to 1 day ahead.

TIP Instead of shaping the tortillas into taco shapes, fry them flat and serve the fish on top of the taco canapé. You can also use store-bought round tortilla chips instead of frying your own. Slice the top of the lime off so it's flat (rather than V-shaped as it is in the main recipe) and rest the flat taco on top for serving.

quesadillas and margaritas

MAKES 2½ TO 3 DOZEN

My take on the ever-popular quesadilla involves layering it with avocado, Brie, roasted red peppers, and Kalamata olives. Topped with a tangy tomatillo salsa, it's a new spin on a favorite that becomes a cool presentation when paired with a classic margarita served in shot glasses or in a mini Patròn bottle and sipped through a straw. Tomatillos come in a papery husk, so be sure to remove the husks and then rinse the tomatillos under cool water before dicing them.

FOR THE SALSA
1¼ cups diced tomatillos
2 garlic cloves, finely minced
2 tablespoons finely chopped fresh cilantro
1 tablespoon extra-virgin olive oil
1 tablespoon fresh lime juice
1 teaspoon finely chopped red onion (or ½ scallion, finely chopped)
1 teaspoon finely chopped jalapeño pepper
½ teaspoon sugar
Coarse salt and freshly ground black pepper

FOR THE MARGARITAS
¼ cup sugar
1¼ cups fresh lime juice (from about 15 limes)
¾ cup plus 2 tablespoons tequila
¼ cup orange liqueur, such as Cointreau, Grand Marnier, or Triple Sec
½ teaspoon coarse salt

FOR THE QUESADILLAS
8 6-inch flour tortillas
1 ripe avocado
2 teaspoons fresh lemon juice
Coarse salt and freshly ground black pepper
2 tablespoons finely chopped pitted Kalamata olives
2 tablespoons finely chopped jarred roasted red peppers
8 ounces Brie cheese, rind removed and sliced into ⅛-inch-thick strips

salsa | In a medium bowl, mix together the tomatillos, garlic, cilantro, olive oil, lime juice, red onion, jalapeño, and sugar. Stir in salt and pepper to taste, cover with plastic wrap, and set aside at room temperature for at least 20 minutes or up to a few hours.

margaritas | Place ¼ cup water and the sugar in a small saucepan over medium heat. Stir until the sugar is dissolved, and then raise the heat to medium-high and cook until the mixture comes to a simmer. Turn off the heat and pour the simple syrup into a small glass or a liquid measuring cup. Cover it with plastic wrap and refrigerate until thoroughly chilled, at least 2 hours.

In a small pitcher, mix ¼ cup of the chilled simple syrup with the lime juice, tequila, orange liqueur, and salt. Cover with plastic wrap and refrigerate until serving. (Save the rest of the simple syrup, covered, in the refrigerator for another time; it will keep for a few weeks.)

quesadillas | Preheat the oven to 350°F.

Heat a ridged grill pan over medium-high heat. Place a tortilla on the pan and cook on each side until there are grill marks, 30 seconds to 1 minute per side. Repeat with the remaining tortillas.

Halve and pit the avocado. Scoop the flesh from the skin and place it in a medium bowl. Use a fork to mash it with the lemon juice, and then season with a little salt and pepper.

Lay 1 grilled tortilla on a cutting board. Spread with one fourth of the avocado mixture, and then sprinkle with one fourth of the olives and one fourth of the red peppers. Place one fourth of the sliced Brie over the peppers and top with another tortilla. Repeat with the remaining tortillas and filling.

Place the quesadillas on a baking sheet and bake in the oven until the cheese is melted, 3 to 5 minutes. Let the quesadillas cool for 5 minutes, and then transfer them to a wire rack to cool completely. Once cool, place them on a cutting board. Using a 2-inch round cookie cutter, stamp out 8 to 9 rounds from each quesadilla.

Place the 2-inch quesadillas on a baking sheet and bake until warmed through, about 10 minutes.

serve | Pour the margarita mixture into a cocktail shaker. Add some ice cubes, cover the shaker, and shake vigorously to chill. Use a cocktail strainer to strain the margarita mixture, dividing it among thirty to thirty-six shot glasses or mini Patròn bottles.

Remove the quesadillas from the oven and place them on a platter. Top each with a spoonful of tomatillo salsa. Serve with a margarita shot.

MAKE AHEAD The salsa can be refrigerated up to 1 day in advance. Let it sit at room temperature for 20 minutes before serving.

The quesadillas can be made a few hours in advance. Leave them out at room temperature and rewarm them in a hot oven just before serving.

spicy tomato salsa
MAKES 1½ CUPS

This classic tomato salsa is excellent with the Quesadillas and Margaritas (opposite) or a simple bowl of tortilla chips. To peel tomatoes, either use a serrated vegetable peeler or slice a small X in the bottom of each tomato, blanch in boiling water for 30 seconds (longer if the tomatoes aren't very ripe), and then plunge in ice water to chill. Peel the skin away and discard.

2 medium tomatoes, peeled, seeded, and finely chopped
¼ cup finely chopped fresh cilantro leaves
2 serrano chiles, seeded and finely chopped
1 garlic clove, finely minced
¼ teaspoon finely minced red onion (or shallot)
3 tablespoons extra-virgin olive oil
2 teaspoons fresh lime juice
Coarse salt and freshly ground black pepper

Place the tomatoes, cilantro, chiles, garlic, and red onion in a medium bowl. Stir in the olive oil, lime juice, and some salt and pepper to taste. Cover the bowl with plastic wrap, and set aside at room temperature for at least 30 minutes or refrigerate for up 2 days before using (let the salsa sit at room temperature before serving).

corn soup and bacon

MAKES 2 DOZEN

I was catering a wedding for clients who had their hearts set on serving the corn soup from The Ivy in Los Angeles, so I sent a friend to the restaurant and had him ship the soup back to us! The version we then created was so delicious that it's now one of our favorite soups. Try using fresh in-season ingredients when you can.

FOR THE SOUP

4 ears corn in their husks (or 6 cups frozen sweet white corn)
½ jalapeño pepper, halved, seeded, and deribbed
2 tablespoons unsalted butter
1 medium sweet onion, such as Maui or Vidalia, chopped
2 celery stalks, chopped
1½ medium carrots, chopped
2 garlic cloves, smashed
3 fresh thyme sprigs
2 fresh rosemary sprigs
½ bay leaf
1½ quarts (6 cups) chicken broth, vegetable broth, or water
⅓ teaspoon finely chopped chipotle chile, canned in adobo sauce (optional)
Coarse salt and freshly ground black pepper

FOR THE BACON

6 thick-cut bacon strips (preferably double-smoked)

soup | Preheat the oven to 350°F.

Place the corn and jalapeño pieces (cut side down) on a parchment-paper-lined rimmed baking sheet. Roast until the corn is fragrant and the husks are dried out and until the skin of the jalapeño is blistered and starting to peel off, about 30 minutes. (If using frozen corn, just roast the jalapeño on a square of aluminum foil.) Remove the baking sheet from the oven and set aside to cool.

Remove and discard the corn husks. Slice the kernels off the cobs and place them in a bowl. Save the cobs and set aside. Peel the skin off the jalapeño and set aside.

In a large pot, melt 1 tablespoon of the butter over medium heat. Add half of the chopped onion and cook, stirring often, until just translucent (don't let it brown), 3 to 4 minutes. Stir in half of the celery, all the carrots, and the garlic, thyme, rosemary, bay leaf, and broth. Add the reserved corncobs and bring to a boil over medium-high heat. Then reduce the heat to medium-low and simmer gently until the carrots are very tender, about 40 minutes. Strain the soup through a fine-mesh sieve into a large bowl and set aside. Discard the solids.

In a large clean pot, melt the remaining 1 tablespoon butter over medium heat. Add the remaining onion and celery and cook until soft but not browned, 4 to 6 minutes. Stir in the roasted corn kernels and the jalapeño, and pour in the corn broth. Bring to a boil over medium-high heat. Reduce the heat to medium-low and simmer for 10 minutes. Remove from the heat and set aside to cool for 15 minutes.

Purée half of the soup in a blender and then strain it through a fine-mesh sieve into a clean pot. Repeat with the remaining soup. Stir in the chipotle chile (if using), and season to taste with salt and pepper. Set aside.

bacon | Preheat the oven to 375°F.

To make the bacon extra-flat for presentation, bake it under bricks: Wrap two or three bricks in aluminum foil. Place the bacon strips on a parchment-paper-lined rimmed baking sheet. Lay the bricks on top of the bacon, making sure that each slice is completely covered. Bake until the bacon is crisp, 15 to 20 minutes. Remove the pan from the oven and set aside to cool for 20 minutes. Then remove the bricks and slice each strip crosswise into 4 equal pieces.

serve | Heat the oven to 350°F. Place the bacon pieces on a parchment-paper-lined baking sheet and bake until warm and sizzling, 3 to 5 minutes. In a clean pot, rewarm the soup. Divide the soup among twenty-four small glasses or bowls. Let a piece of bacon rest against the side or on the rim of each soup cup.

MAKE AHEAD The cooked soup can be refrigerated for 1 day before serving, or frozen for up to 3 weeks.

The cooked bacon can be refrigerated in an airtight container for 1 day before serving.

> TIP For extra-thick bacon slices, buy a slab of bacon and slice it yourself (or ask your butcher to slice it for you). Wrap leftover slab bacon in plastic wrap, place it in a resealable freezer bag, and freeze it for up to 6 months.

beer and pretzels

MAKES 3 DOZEN

Soft pretzels are not considered a fancy party food, but shrunken down to half-dollar-sized portions, the traditional ballpark fare turns into something chic and completely irresistible. Even though women plan many of the parties we put together, they're always conscious of what would make the men happy. These rich and buttery pretzels, paired with beer, fit the bill.

½ cup warm (110°F.) water
1 tablespoon active dry yeast
4 teaspoons (packed) light brown sugar
1 tablespoon unsalted butter, melted
3 cups all-purpose flour, plus extra for kneading
  and rolling
½ teaspoon flaky sea salt, such as Maldon
1 teaspoon vegetable oil
Nonstick pan spray
½ teaspoon baking soda
2 large eggs
Kosher salt
¼ cup Dijon mustard (optional)
3 bottles chilled beer, such as Pilsner or porter

Pour the warm water into the bowl of a stand mixer. Add the yeast and brown sugar, and whisk together until the sugar is dissolved and the water is cloudy. Set aside until the mixture is foamy, about 5 minutes.

Add the melted butter, followed by the flour, to the yeast mixture. Sprinkle the sea salt on top, and using the paddle attachment, mix the ingredients together until they're well combined, 2 to 3 minutes.

Remove the bowl from the mixer and scrape the dough out onto a lightly floured work surface. Knead the dough by hand until it forms a ball, 2 to 4 minutes. Grease a large bowl with the oil and place the dough ball in the bowl. Turn the dough to coat it. Cover the bowl with plastic wrap and set it aside until the dough has doubled in size, about 1 hour.

Preheat the oven to 400°F. Line two baking sheets with parchment paper and lightly coat the paper with nonstick pan spray.

Press your fingers into the center of the dough ball to deflate it, and then use kitchen shears to divide it into 36 pieces the size of Ping Pong balls. Roll each piece into a ball, and then transfer them to a lightly floured work surface. Use both hands to roll each ball into a 6-inch-long rope of even thickness. Form the rope into a pretzel shape by taking the left end and crossing it over the midsection, creating an upper-left-hand loop. Repeat with the right end of the rope, crossing it over the midsection, creating an upper-right loop. Adjust the ends so they overlap and hang nicely off the pretzel. Place the shaped pretzels on the prepared baking sheets.

In a medium pot, bring 4 cups water to a simmer over medium-high heat. Add the baking soda and then add a few pretzels to the pot. Once they rise to the top and are puffy, after about 1 minute, use a slotted spoon to transfer them back to the oiled parchment paper, leaving at least 1 inch between pretzels on the baking sheet. Repeat with the remaining pretzels.

In a small bowl, whisk the eggs together with a pinch of kosher salt and 2 teaspoons water. Use a pastry brush to coat the pretzels with a thin layer of the egg wash. Sprinkle the tops of the pretzels with some kosher salt, and then bake the pretzels until they're golden brown, 4 to 5 minutes. Remove from the oven and let cool for a few minutes before transferring them to a wire rack to cool completely.

Preheat the oven to 350°F.

Place the pretzels on a parchment-paper-lined baking sheet and tent loosely with aluminum foil. Warm in the oven for 3 to 5 minutes. Remove the pretzels from the oven and immediately transfer them to a serving platter. Dab each pretzel with a little mustard (if using) before serving with chilled miniature pilsners or mugs of beer.

MAKE AHEAD The pretzels can be baked, cooled, and then frozen in gallon-sized resealable freezer bags up to 2 weeks before serving. Defrost overnight at room temperature and then rewarm following the serving instructions.

TIP Instead of making classic pretzel shapes, you can simply divide the large dough ball into 6 smaller balls, roll each into a rope and then cut it into 6 1½-inch pretzel sticks.

LOLLIPOPS, CONES, + MORE

Artichoke Lollipops | Mango-Shrimp Lollipops

Watermelon-Mint Lollipops | Butternut Squash Lollipops

Chicken-Parmesan Lollipops | Lamb and Mint Pesto Lollipops

Tuna Tartare Plantain Cones | Crab in Potato Cones

Grilled Vegetables in Plantain Cones | Caviar Cones

Grape Leaf Cigarettes | Chicken Nori Cigarettes

I'VE BEEN TOLD MORE THAN ONCE THAT THERE IS AN *Alice in Wonderland* aspect to my food, which I take as a great compliment. This chapter is all about presenting food in unexpected and whimsical ways, from butternut squash "lollipops" to tuna tartare "ice cream cones" and chicken nori "cigarettes."

In this chapter you'll find shrimp "lollipops," "ice cream" cones made of potato cones and a scoop of caviar, and grape leaf "cigarettes" served in chic silver cigarette boxes. These are fun hors d'oeuvres that always ramp up the energy at a party the instant that they're presented.

artichoke lollipops

MAKES 2 DOZEN

An artichoke heart provides for a perfectly round lollipop in this simple and pretty hors d'oeuvre. A lemony olive oil marinade and a dot of homemade hollandaise (it takes only 30 seconds in the blender) give the artichokes a wonderfully bright flavor. *(Pictured on page 85.)*

FOR THE HOLLANDAISE
3 large egg yolks
2 tablespoons fresh lemon juice
2 drops hot sauce
½ teaspoon kosher salt
Pinch of freshly ground black pepper
½ cup clarified butter (see Tips)

FOR THE ARTICHOKES
24 whole artichoke hearts (from about 4 14-ounce cans,
    preferably Rienzi brand), drained
¼ cup extra-virgin olive oil
Grated zest of ½ lemon
½ teaspoon kosher salt
¼ teaspoon freshly ground black pepper
24 lollipop sticks (or 4-inch-long wood skewers)

FOR SERVING
24 small fresh dill fronds

hollandaise | Place the egg yolks, lemon juice, hot sauce, salt, and pepper in a blender jar and blend until frothy. With the blender running, drizzle in the clarified butter in a slow stream until the sauce is thick and bright yellow. Pour the sauce into a plastic container, cover, and chill until serving.

artichokes | Place each artichoke heart on a cutting board and slice away the stem end and any of the remaining leafy part so you're left with a flat disk. Line a rimmed baking sheet with plastic wrap and place the artichokes on top. Drizzle the olive oil over the artichokes and then sprinkle with the lemon zest, salt, and pepper.

serve | Spread ⅛ teaspoon of the chilled hollandaise over the flat surface of each artichoke round. Finish with a dill frond. Insert a lollipop stick into the edge of each artichoke, pushing it into the center. Cover the baking sheet with plastic wrap and refrigerate for 30 minutes. Then place the lollipops on a platter or stand them upright using a customized Styrofoam tray (see page 181), and serve.

MAKE AHEAD The hollandaise can be made up to 1 day ahead.

The artichokes can be cut and seasoned up to 2 days before serving.

TIPS To make ½ cup clarified butter, simply melt 10 tablespoons butter in a small saucepan. Let the solids settle to the bottom, and pour the golden clarified butter off the top, leaving the white solids behind.

If the hollandaise is too thick to spread easily, add warm water, 1 teaspoon at a time, until the consistency is like mayonnaise.

mango-shrimp lollipops

MAKES 2 DOZEN

We served this twist on the classic shrimp cocktail at a party hosted by Will and Jada Smith. After the shrimp marinate in a sweet and spicy sauce made with mango, fresh ginger, lime juice, and chipotle chiles, they go for a quick turn in the oven, where they naturally curl into a nice, round lollipop shape. We often pair these with the Artichoke Lollipops (page 83) for a great presentation.

2 very ripe mangos, peeled, seeded, and roughly chopped
½ cup cream of coconut, such as Coco Lopez
2 garlic cloves, roughly chopped
1 canned chipotle chile in adobo sauce, roughly chopped
2 tablespoons fresh lime juice
1 tablespoon dark rum
1 tablespoon finely grated peeled fresh ginger
1 teaspoon Tabasco sauce
½ teaspoon ground coriander
½ teaspoon ground cumin
1 teaspoon salt
2 tablespoons finely chopped fresh cilantro
24 large shrimp (21–25 shrimp per pound), peeled and deveined
24 lollipop sticks (or 4-inch-long wood skewers)

Place the mangos, cream of coconut, garlic, chipotle, lime juice, rum, ginger, Tabasco, coriander, cumin, and salt in the bowl of a food processor and process until smooth.

Pour the marinade into a resealable gallon-sized bag, add the cilantro, seal, and shake to combine. Add the shrimp to the marinade, seal, and marinate in the refrigerator for at least 30 minutes or up to 2 hours.

Preheat the oven to 350°F.

Remove the shrimp from the marinade, letting the excess drip back into the bag. Place the shrimp on a parchment-paper-lined rimmed baking sheet so that they are all facing the same direction. Cook until the shrimp turn pink, about 15 minutes, and then set aside to cool completely.

Skewer each shrimp on a lollipop stick or a skewer, and serve on a platter. To serve the lollipops upright, fill a deep rectangular tray with dried black beans (or a piece of Styrofoam) and insert the skewers in the beans.

MAKE AHEAD The mango marinade can be refrigerated for up to 4 days before using, or frozen for up to 1 month.

The shrimp can be peeled and deveined 1 day before serving, and can be cooked and then refrigerated up to 8 hours ahead of serving.

> **TIP** For a glossy finish, set aside a few tablespoons of the marinade before adding the shrimp to the bag. Brush a little on each shrimp after they're skewered and just before serving.

VARIATION
classic shrimp cocktail lollipops

To make a classic shrimp cocktail, toss the shrimp in a large bowl with some extra-virgin olive oil, salt, and pepper and bake and skewer them following the instructions above. Finish them with a dot of cocktail sauce, and serve.

watermelon-mint lollipops

MAKES 2 DOZEN

Watermelon lollipops are stunning, refreshing, and simple to execute. To create a sophisticated version of the vodka-spiked watermelon most of us recall (hazily) from our youth, we soaked the watermelon with an orange-flavored liqueur.

1 2- to 3-pound seedless watermelon, such as
   Sugar Baby
¼ cup Grand Marnier (or other orange liqueur)
24 lollipop sticks (or 4-inch-long wood skewers)
24 small fresh mint leaves

Slice the watermelon flesh into ⅓-inch-thick pieces. Use a round 1½-inch cookie cutter to stamp out 24 small rounds.

Pour the liqueur in a 9 × 13-inch baking dish. Place the watermelon rounds in the liqueur and let them soak for 1 minute. Then turn them over so the other side soaks in some liqueur too, for at least 1 minute or up to 8 hours.

Insert a lollipop stick or a skewer into the edge of each round so it reaches the center. Lay a mint leaf on the center of each watermelon round. Place the sticks on a platter, or fill a deep rectangular tray with dried black beans or a piece of Styrofoam to hold the skewers upright, and serve.

MAKE AHEAD The watermelon can be shaped and soaked up to 8 hours ahead, and can be skewered and finished with the mint leaves up to 1 hour in advance. Refrigerate, covered with plastic wrap, until serving.

> **TIP** For a spring or summer party, it's fun to serve flower-shaped watermelon lollipops. Use a flower-shaped cookie cutter to stamp out the shapes. You can even mix up the colors, using yellow seedless watermelon as well as pink.

VARIATION
fresh fruit lollipops

Pineapple, honeydew melon, and canteloupe all make for delicious lollipops. For an adult flavor, soak them in sugar-cane liquor, tequila, or rum before skewering and serving.

butternut squash lollipops

MAKES 2 DOZEN

The bright orange color of butternut squash makes this lollipop really stand out. An apple and walnut oil–seasoned chèvre center counters the squash's sweetness, while a tender round of leek finishes the look. This lollipop is best served in the fall and winter, when squash and apples are at their peak flavor. Use any leftover squash for soup or purée it for a ravioli filling.

FOR THE CHÈVRE FILLING
2 ounces fresh chèvre (goat cheese)
1 medium Granny Smith apple, peeled and grated on the large holes of a box grater
2 teaspoons walnut oil
⅓ teaspoon sugar
⅛ teaspoon ground cinnamon
Pinch of salt

FOR THE SQUASH
1 large or 2 medium butternut squash, skin removed with a vegetable peeler
1 2-inch piece fresh ginger, peeled and grated
Flaky sea salt, such as Maldon
24 lollipop sticks (or 4-inch-long wood skewers)

FOR THE LEEKS
1 small leek, green top only

chèvre filling | In a medium bowl, mix the chèvre, apple, walnut oil, sugar, cinnamon, and salt. Cover the bowl with plastic wrap and chill for at least 1 hour.

squash | Preheat the oven to 350°F.

Place the squash on a cutting board and trim off the root and stem ends. Slice the squash cross-wise into ½-inch-thick rounds. Set the solid slices (the ones without seeds or fibers) in a single layer on a rimmed baking sheet. (Wrap the remaining squash, with fibers and seeds, in plastic wrap and refrigerate for up to 5 days for another use.)

Pour in just enough water to cover the bottom of the baking sheet. Sprinkle the ginger over the squash and cover the baking sheet tightly with a sheet of aluminum foil. Roast until the squash is tender, about 40 minutes. Remove the baking sheet from the oven. Use tongs to carefully remove the foil, and sprinkle the squash with some sea salt. Set aside.

Once the squash is cool, scrape away any obvious bits of ginger. Use a 1½-inch round cookie cutter to stamp out rounds from each piece of squash, and then use a ½-inch round cookie cutter to stamp a smaller round from each of the squash centers. You will need only the larger circles; refrigerate the smaller rounds in an airtight container for up to 3 days.

Fit a pastry bag with a round tip (or if using disposable pastry bags, snip ¼ inch from the bottom of the bag to create a small opening) and fill the bag with the chèvre mixture. Pipe the chèvre into the center of each squash circle.

leeks | Place a bowl of ice water on your work surface. Bring a pot of water to a boil. Add the leek

(recipe continues)

greens and blanch until they wilt, about 1 minute. Drain, and transfer the leek greens to the ice water to stop the cooking. Remove from the ice water, place on a kitchen towel, and pat dry.

Use a ½-inch round cookie cutter to stamp out small rounds from the leek greens. Place a leek round on each side of the chèvre filling within the butternut squash. Press the leek onto the chèvre so it stays in place.

serve | Insert a lollipop stick into the edge of the squash so it reaches halfway through the middle. Place the lollipops on a platter or stand them upright using a customized Styrofoam tray (see page 181), and serve.

VARIATIONS

For a sweet finish, dip the butternut squash lollipop in maple syrup and coat the edges with crushed pistachios. Or use blue cheese in the middle instead of the chèvre. For kids, put a marshmallow in the middle!

MAKE AHEAD The seasoned chèvre can be prepared up to 2 days before serving.

The lollipops can be assembled and refrigerated up to 1 day before serving. Let the lollipops sit out at room temperature for at least 20 minutes before serving.

> **TIPS** Butternut squash with long necks and small round bases yield the most squash to make these hors d'oeuvres.
>
> For a dramatic presentation, fill a deep rectangular tray with enough dried black beans to stand the skewers upright.

chicken-parmesan lollipops

MAKES 2 DOZEN

Once chicken Parmesan is on a lollipop stick, it instantly works, looking stylish while tasting delicious. This is a great kid-friendly hors d'oeuvre that adults gravitate toward, too.

FOR THE MARINADE
½ cup buttermilk
½ cup dark beer
½ teaspoon coarse salt
½ teaspoon freshly ground black pepper
6 3-ounce thin-cut chicken cutlets

FOR FRYING
2 cups peanut oil
5 large eggs
1 cup all-purpose flour
1 teaspoon coarse salt
½ teaspoon freshly ground black pepper
3 cups panko breadcrumbs
1½ cups freshly grated Parmigiano-Reggiano cheese

FOR SERVING
¼ cup store-bought marinara sauce
1 4-ounce ball fresh salted mozzarella, sliced into 12 rounds, each round divided into 2 circles using a 1¼-inch round cookie cutter
24 lollipop sticks (or 4-inch-long wood skewers)
24 flat-leaf parsley leaves

marinade | Whisk the buttermilk, beer, salt, and pepper together in a large bowl. Add the chicken to the marinade, turn to coat, cover the bowl with plastic wrap, and refrigerate for at least 2 hours or overnight.

frying | In a large, deep skillet, heat the oil to 350°F. over medium heat.

While the oil is heating, whisk the eggs together in a medium bowl. Whisk the flour, salt, and pepper together in another medium or large bowl, and mix the panko and Parmesan together in a medium bowl.

Remove the cutlets from the marinade, letting the excess drip off. Dredge 1 chicken cutlet through the seasoned flour, making sure both sides are evenly coated and tapping off the excess. Dip the floured cutlet in the egg mixture, letting any excess drip back into the bowl, and then press both sides into the panko/Parmesan mixture. Place the breaded chicken cutlet on a baking sheet and repeat with the remaining cutlets.

Place the chicken cutlets in the skillet (if the oil has become too hot, reduce the heat to medium-low and wait for the temperature to come down before frying), and fry them on both sides until they are golden brown and cooked through, about 4 minutes total (you may need to fry the chicken in batches). Use tongs to transfer the chicken to a paper-towel-lined plate to drain and cool completely.

Set the cooled fried chicken on a cutting board. Use a 1¼-inch round cookie cutter to stamp 24 rounds from the chicken cutlets, and place them on a parchment-paper-lined baking sheet.

(recipe continues)

serve | Preheat the oven to 350°F.

Spread ⅛ teaspoon of the tomato sauce on one side of each chicken round and cover the sauce with a piece of cheese. Place the chicken in the oven and bake until the cheese begins to melt, 2 to 3 minutes. Remove from the oven, and use tongs to hold each round while you insert a lollipop stick or a skewer into the bottom edge of the chicken and halfway through the middle. Finish with a parsley leaf. Place on a platter, or use a customized Styrofoam tray (see page 181), or fill a deep rectangular tray with dried heirloom Italian beans to hold the skewers upright, and serve.

MAKE AHEAD Breaded uncooked chicken breasts can be wrapped in plastic wrap and kept frozen in a resealable gallon-sized freezer bag for up to 2 weeks. Thaw overnight in the refrigerator before frying.

TIP Buy prepared chicken Parmesan from your favorite Italian restaurant or market and cut rounds out with a cookie cutter for the same effect in a *lot* less time.

A Sophisticated Tailgating Tray | Game day doesn't have to be about messy nachos and chicken wings. Here are a few ideas for appetizers to make tailgating as tasteful as it is fun.

- Chicken-Parmesan Lollipops (page 91)
- Beer and Pretzels (page 78)
- Hot Dogs (page 45)
- Beef and Beer (page 70)
- Meatball Heros (page 35)
- Baked Beans (page 26)

lamb and mint pesto lollipops

MAKES 2 DOZEN

"Individual lamb rib chops" used to be a dreaded hors d'oeuvre request because I always found the sight of a guest left holding a lamb bone unappealing. My solution is to serve rounds of boneless lamb loin as lollipops. I like using New Zealand lamb loins because they're the smallest.

FOR THE PESTO
1 cup (packed) fresh basil leaves
1 cup (packed) fresh mint leaves
¼ cup toasted shelled pistachios (optional)
2 garlic cloves, smashed
2 tablespoons fresh lemon juice
1 teaspoon kosher salt
½ teaspoon freshly ground black pepper
½ cup extra-virgin olive oil

FOR THE LAMB
2 1-pound lamb loins
Kosher salt and freshly ground black pepper
1 cup finely chopped fresh chervil (or parsley) leaves
1 cup chopped fresh chives
24 lollipop sticks (or 4-inch-long wood skewers)

pesto | Place the basil, mint, pistachios (if using), garlic, lemon juice, salt, and pepper in the bowl of a food processor and process until roughly combined, about 30 seconds. With the processor running, drizzle in the olive oil and process until the sauce comes together, about 2 minutes. Refrigerate in an airtight container until serving.

lamb | Season the lamb loins with salt and pepper. Mix the chervil and chives together in a small bowl, and then turn half of the mixture out onto a work surface, spreading the mixture out into a strip about the length of the lamb. Roll the lamb in the herbs to evenly coat the surface. Tightly wrap the loins in plastic wrap, and tightly twist the ends of the plastic to seal. Place both loins on a rimmed baking sheet and place in the freezer until completely frozen, about 8 hours.

Preheat the oven to 350°F.

Remove the lamb from the freezer and unwrap each loin. Heat a grill pan over medium-high heat (or a charcoal or gas grill to medium-high heat), place one lamb loin in the pan, and grill it on all sides until it has grill marks, about 4 minutes total. Place the loin on a rimmed baking sheet and grill the other lamb loin.

Roast the lamb in the oven until it reads 130° to 135°F. on an instant-read thermometer, 15 to 18 minutes. Let the lamb rest for 4 minutes before slicing it into ½-inch-thick rounds (12 slices per loin).

serve | Use tongs to hold each round while you insert a lollipop stick or a skewer into the edge of the lamb, reaching halfway through. Spoon some mint pesto on the top edge of each piece of lamb and then dip the pesto-covered edge in the remaining chervil and chives. Place the lollipops on a platter or stand them upright using a customized Styrofoam tray (see page 181), and serve.

MAKE AHEAD The pesto can be refrigerated in an airtight container for up to 4 days. Bring it to room temperature before serving.

The herb-coated lamb loins can be frozen for up to 1 month. They can be grilled up to 8 hours before finishing them in the oven and serving.

> **TIP** If your butcher doesn't have lamb loins, you can buy two 9-bone racks of lamb and separate the loin from the rack by following the contour of the bone with a sharp boning knife. Remove the silverskin and the excess fat, and proceed with coating the lamb in the herbs.

tuna tartare plantain cones

MAKES 2 DOZEN

I was so inspired by a certain restaurateur's salmon tartare–topped cornmeal cone that I had to create one of my own by taking the concept a step further. I shape a thin strip of plantain into a cone and fry it to use as the cup, then fill the cup with an herbaceous tuna tartare. It's one of the first hors d'oeuvres I ever served on a clear acrylic tray, which makes the cones look as if they're floating through a room (we did this at Tom Petty's book party).

FOR THE PLANTAIN CONES
6 cups peanut oil
3 green plantains, ends removed, peeled
Nonstick pan spray
Kosher salt

FOR THE TUNA TARTARE
1½ tablespoons fresh lime juice
1 tablespoon extra-virgin olive oil
¼ teaspoon adobo sauce from a can of chipotle chiles in adobo sauce
1 tablespoon finely minced shallot
1 garlic clove, finely minced
1 tablespoon finely chopped fresh cilantro leaves
1 tablespoon finely chopped fresh chives
8 ounces sushi-grade tuna, diced into ¼-inch cubes
½ teaspoon kosher salt
¼ teaspoon freshly ground black pepper

FOR SERVING
Chopped fresh chives

plantain cones | In a large heavy-bottomed pot, heat the oil to 350°F. over medium heat. Using a mandoline or a very sharp chef's knife, slice the plantains lengthwise into twenty-four ¹⁄₁₆-inch-thick strips. Coat sixteen #800 heatproof round pastry tips with pan spray. Starting at the narrow pointed end of a tip, wrap a plantain strip in a spiral up and around the tip, slightly overlapping the layers, until you get to the top. Use scissors to cut away the overhang. Repeat with three more pastry tips. Fit each plantain-wrapped tip into another tip (the second tip holds it in place), and fry until the plantain is golden, 2 to 3 minutes. Line a plate with paper towels, and using a slotted spoon or a frying spider, transfer the cones to the plate to cool completely before removing the tips.

While the first batch cools, repeat with the remaining eight tips and 4 more plantain strips.

Remove the tips from the first cooled batch, sprinkle the cones with salt, and set them aside. Remove the second batch from the oil and set it aside to cool. Repeat 4 times with the remaining plantain slices.

tuna tartare | Whisk the lime juice, olive oil, adobo sauce, shallot, garlic, cilantro, and chives together in a medium bowl. Add the tuna and toss gently to coat with the sauce. Season with the salt and pepper.

serve | Fill each plantain cone with 1 teaspoon of the tartare. Place a few chives on top, and serve immediately. The cones can be presented on a platter or served in small shot glasses to keep them upright.

MAKE AHEAD The tuna can be diced up to 8 hours before serving, but do not mix the tuna with the sauce until right before serving.

> **TIP** Use store-bought plantain chips instead of making your own plantain cones.

crab in potato cones

MAKES 2 DOZEN

This cone is always a big hit, as the crab salad is absolutely delicious, especially paired with the crisp potato chip-like cone. We first served the crab cones at Milk Studios, a fabulous New York City venue where we've catered to rock stars and European princesses.

FOR THE POTATO CONES
6 cups peanut oil
2 large russet potatoes
Nonstick pan spray

FOR THE CRAB
2 Key limes
8 ounces jumbo lump crabmeat (preferably fresh and unpasteurized), picked over for shells
2 tablespoons fresh Key lime juice
1 tablespoon mirin (rice wine)
1 teaspoon finely chopped fresh chives
1 teaspoon finely minced fresh jalapeño pepper
½ teaspoon flaky sea salt, such as Maldon

potato cones | In a large heavy-bottomed pot, heat the oil to 350°F. over medium heat. Using a mandoline or a very sharp chef's knife, slice the potatoes lengthwise into twenty-four $1/16$-inch-thick strips. Spray them with pan spray. Coat sixteen #800 heatproof pastry tips with pan spray. Starting at the narrow pointed end of a tip, wrap a potato strip in a spiral up and around the tip, slightly overlapping the layers until you get to the top. Use scissors to cut away the overhang. Repeat with three more pastry tips. Fit each potato-wrapped tip into another tip (the second tip holds it in place), and fry until the potato is golden, about 30 seconds. Line a plate with paper towels, and using a slotted spoon or a frying spider, transfer the cones to the plate to cool completely before removing the tips.

While the first batch cools, repeat with the remaining eight tips and 4 more potato strips.

Remove the tips from the first cooled batch and set the fried potato cones aside. Remove the second batch from the oil and set it aside to cool. Repeat 4 times with the remaining potato strips.

crab | Slice off the top and bottom from each lime. Stand each lime upright and slice off the peel in strips, working from top to bottom, so the white pith is removed and the fruit is exposed. Using a sharp paring knife, slice between the white membranes to dislodge the lime segments. Place 12 segments in a small bowl. Add the crabmeat, lime juice, mirin, chives, and jalapeño, season with the sea salt, and stir gently to combine.

serve | Spoon some of the crab mixture into each cone, and serve on a platter or in small shot glasses to keep them upright.

MAKE AHEAD The potato cones can be made up to 4 days in advance and stored in an airtight container in a cool, dry place.

The crab salad can be refrigerated for up to 2 hours before serving.

> **TIP** Sturdy thick-cut, ridged, or waffle-cut potato chips can be used in place of the potato cones.

grilled vegetables in plantain cones

MAKES 2 DOZEN

I always make sure to offer one vegetable hors d'oeuvre for every seafood, poultry, and meat hors d'oeuvre. While it does take a little time and patience to place the veggie bundles inside each cone, the payoff here is worth it—these wonderfully light and crunchy cones will please all your guests, even the die-hard meat-eaters.

FOR THE TOMATO AND PEPPER PURÉE
1 cup sun-dried tomatoes (dry, not packed in oil),
    soaked in warm water for 20 minutes
¼ cup jarred roasted red pepper strips
2 tablespoons extra-virgin olive oil
1 tablespoon balsamic vinegar
¼ teaspoon coarse salt
¼ teaspoon freshly ground black pepper

FOR THE VEGETABLES
1 large carrot, trimmed to 3-inch length
1 medium yellow bell pepper
½ cup extra-virgin olive oil
1½ teaspoons coarse salt
½ teaspoon freshly ground black pepper
1 large portobello mushroom, gills scraped away
24 asparagus spears, trimmed to 4-inch lengths

FOR SERVING
24 cooked plantain cones (page 96)
Thinly sliced papaya, for garnish

tomato and pepper purée | Drain the tomatoes and place them in a food processor. Add the roasted peppers, olive oil, balsamic vinegar, salt, and pepper, and process until puréed and thick. Set aside.

vegetables | Slice the carrot lengthwise into ⅛-inch-thick planks. Place the yellow bell pepper upright on a cutting board and slice down from the stem, working your way around the seeds in the center, so you end up with 4 long strips.

In a small bowl, whisk together the olive oil, salt, and pepper. Use a pastry brush to brush the seasoned oil over all sides of the carrots, yellow bell pepper strips, mushroom, and asparagus spears.

Heat a grill pan over high heat, and grill the vegetables (in batches) until both sides have grill marks, about 1 to 3 minutes per side. The vegetables should remain al dente.

Place the carrots on a work surface and slice them in half widthwise (so you have six 1½-inch-long strips) and then lengthwise into ⅛-inch-thick sticks. Repeat with the yellow bell peppers. Cut off the tips from the asparagus stalks (you can save the stalks for another use). Trim away the rounded edges of the mushroom and then slice the square in half widthwise and then lengthwise to form ⅛-inch-thick strips. You should end up with at least 24 strips (or tips) of each vegetable.

serve | Separate the vegetables into 24 bundles, each with 1 strip (or tip) of each vegetable. Place each bundle inside a plantain cone and top with a small dollop of tomato and pepper purée. The cones can be presented on a platter garnished with papaya slices, or served in small shot glasses to keep them upright.

MAKE AHEAD The tomato and pepper purée can be refrigerated in an airtight container for up to 1 week.

The vegetables can be grilled 1 day in advance. Refrigerate them until 1 hour before serving; then let them sit out at room temperature until you're ready to assemble the cones.

caviar cones

MAKES 2 DOZEN

This is the most elegant cone I make, and also the most difficult. It takes a steady hand to top each potato cone with a perfect scoop of caviar, but the finished effect is fabulous.

¼ **cup whipped cream cheese**
24 **cooked potato cones (page 99)**
3 **ounces caviar, such as American paddlefish**
¼ **cup crème fraîche**

Smear ½ teaspoon of the cream cheese across the top of each cone. Mound ½ teaspoon of the caviar on top of the cream cheese. Place the crème fraîche in a pastry bag fitted with a small metal tip, and pipe a small pearl of crème fraîche on top of the caviar. The cones can be presented on a platter or served in small shot glasses to keep them upright.

> **TIP** Sturdy thick-cut, ridged, or waffle-cut potato chips can be used in place of the potato cones.

grape leaf cigarettes

MAKES 2 DOZEN

I like presenting hors d'oeuvres in pairs, such as the Mango-Shrimp Lollipops (page 84) with the Artichoke Lollipops (page 83). When I came up with the idea for the Chicken Nori Cigarettes (page 105), I wanted them to have a counterpart served alongside. Having spent time in Greece, I thought of grape leaves and the obvious filling of rice, feta, and olives. *HomeStyle* magazine included this hors d'oeuvre in an article about my sexy canapés, and announced that they caused quite a sensation! *(Pictured on page 104.)*

1 tablespoon extra-virgin olive oil
Kosher salt and freshly ground black pepper
1⅓ cups long-grain white rice
1⅓ cups crumbled feta cheese
⅔ cup diced pitted Kalamata olives
½ small red onion, finely minced
6 garlic cloves, finely minced
3 tablespoons finely chopped mixed fresh herbs, such as a combination of basil, mint, oregano, and thyme
24 canned marinated grape leaves

Pour 2 cups of water into a medium saucepan. Add the olive oil, 1 teaspoon salt, and ⅔ teaspoon pepper, and bring to a boil. Stir in the rice, cover, reduce the heat to low, and cook until the rice is tender, 16 to 18 minutes. Transfer the rice to a large plate to cool.

Place the feta, olives, onion, garlic, and chopped herbs in a food processor. Add the cooled rice and pulse 2 to 3 times to roughly chop. Taste for seasoning, and add salt and pepper if needed.

Trim the grape leaves into 3 × 4-inch rectangles. If the stem running up the middle of the leaf is thick, carefully trim it off without cutting through the leaf; this will help make rolling easier. Place ½ tablespoon of the filling lengthwise across the bottom of each grape leaf. Roll tightly from the bottom up to make an even cylinder. Trim the ends.

Serve in a silver cigarette box or a nice cigar box, or fill a silver cup (like a mint julep cup) with dried beans and place the cigarettes in the cup so the tops of the cigarettes rise above the rim of the cup.

MAKE AHEAD The filling can be made up to 2 days ahead and refrigerated.

The grape leaves can be filled and rolled up to 1 day before serving; cover and refrigerate.

chicken nori cigarettes

MAKES 2 DOZEN

This hors d'oeuvre is one of our biggest hits, and the concept has been featured in several magazines as well as *USA Today*. Nori are thin sheets of seaweed, the same kind used to make maki sushi rolls in Japanese restaurants. They can be found in the international aisle of most supermarkets.

Some people find it's easier to make a larger cigar-sized version rather than small cigarettes. To complete the look, present them in a cigar box.

FOR THE FILLING
½ cup dry white wine, such as Sauvignon Blanc
½ cup soy or tamari sauce
1 1-inch piece fresh ginger, peeled
4 ounces boneless, skinless thin-cut chicken cutlets
1 medium carrot, ends trimmed
1 medium red bell pepper
24 fresh chives

FOR THE CIGARETTES
4 sheets nori
1 tablespoon prepared wasabi paste
2 ounces (2 tablespoons) thinly sliced pickled ginger

filling | In a medium saucepan, bring the wine, soy sauce, 1 cup of water, and the fresh ginger to a boil. Reduce the heat to medium-low and add the chicken, making sure the cutlets are completely covered with liquid. Simmer gently until cooked through, 5 to 7 minutes. Remove the chicken from the broth and set aside to cool. Once cool, slice the chicken in half widthwise and then into ⅛-inch-thick strips.

Slice the carrot lengthwise into four or five ⅛-inch-thick planks. Cut the carrot planks in half widthwise, and then slice them lengthwise into ⅛-inch-thick sticks. Place the bell pepper upright on a cutting board and slice down from the stem, working your way around the seeds in the center, so you end up with 4 long strips. Slice the strips in half widthwise and then into ⅛-inch-thick matchsticks to match the carrots. Cut the chives into 4-inch lengths. Separate the vegetables and chives into 24 bundles, each with 1 strip of carrot, pepper, and chive.

cigarettes | Place a small bowl of water next to your work surface. Place the nori on your cutting board, shiny side down, and cut each sheet into six 2 × 4-inch rectangles. Spread a very thin layer of wasabi lengthwise across the bottom quarter of each piece of nori. Lay a vegetable bundle on top of the wasabi. Top with 1 chicken strip and then a few pieces of pickled ginger.

Dip your finger into the water and lightly moisten the top quarter of the nori sheet. Using the tips of your fingers, gently roll the filling in the nori so you end up with an even cylinder. Trim the ends.

serve | Serve in a silver cigarette box or in a nice cigar box, or fill a silver cup (like a mint julep cup) with dried beans and place the cigarettes in the cup so the tops of the cigarettes rise above the rim of the cup.

MAKE AHEAD The chicken can be cooked and the vegetables can be prepared up to 1 day ahead; cover and refrigerate.

The nori can be filled and rolled up to 3 hours ahead. Cover and refrigerate.

CLASSICS
REINTERPRETED

Foie Gras Truffles | Stuffed Mushrooms

Mini Challah Loaves | Lobster-Potato Petit Fours

Salmon Tarts | Pheasant Under Glass

Pigs in Blankets, Two Ways

Potted Shrimp | Deviled Quail Eggs

Vegetable Spring Rolls | BLTs

Turkey Canapés with Stuffing and Cranberry Relish

THERE ARE CERTAIN DISHES THAT SOME PEOPLE JUST *have* to have at their party—such as pigs in blankets, stuffed mushrooms, and deviled eggs. These are classic hors d'oeuvres for a reason: They stand the test of time and remain appealing even when trends and tastes change. They have gone beyond party food and become a part of our culinary vocabulary.

Giving the classics a clever twist is how I make them work with our anything-but-classic approach to hors d'oeuvres. Of course they must look as amazing as they taste, and it is the presentation that often steals the show—like the speckled quail eggs arranged single-file between two rows of deviled eggs, and the BLTs balanced on top of whole tomatoes. While I admit that sometimes it seems to be the accessories that give the dish that "wow" factor, it's the deliciousness of the food, too!

foie gras truffles

MAKES 2 DOZEN

I love how in fancy restaurants, precious and expensive truffles are presented tableside in a small wood box to showcase their incredible fragrance and knobby appearance. I play off this idea by rolling hand-shaped balls of foie gras in powder-fine mushroom dust, which makes them look like cocoa-dusted chocolate truffles. We present them in a wood box with a hinged lid—when we open the top, it acts like a magician's reveal, letting guests discover the treasures inside.

¼ cup (⅓ ounce) dried porcini mushrooms
1 5-ounce piece store-bought foie gras terrine, chilled

Place the mushrooms in a coffee grinder or a small food processor, and grind to a fine powder. Place the powder in a small bowl.

Set an ice pack next to your work surface and place the terrine on top to keep it cold while you make the truffles. Scoop ½ teaspoon from the terrine and roll it into a ball. Roll the ball in the mushroom powder and then place it on a large plate. Repeat with the remaining terrine, cover the truffles with plastic wrap, and then refrigerate them for at least 1 hour before serving.

Let the truffles sit out at room temperature for 10 to 30 minutes before serving (the hotter the room, the less time you want them sitting out).

MAKE AHEAD The truffles can be made 1 day before serving.

stuffed mushrooms

MAKES 2 DOZEN

The idea for this new version of the stuffed mushroom was sparked by the *Alice in Wonderland* image of the caterpillar smoking his hookah on top of the toadstool: A whole mushroom is the base, with a "stuffed" mushroom balanced on top. These were a hit when we served them at Tony Bennett's holiday party.

FOR THE SHIITAKE CHIPS
24 fresh shiitake mushroom caps

FOR THE MORELS
24 small dried morel mushrooms
2 tablespoons unsalted butter
1 small leek, white part only, finely chopped
2 garlic cloves, finely minced
½ cup port wine
2 teaspoons finely chopped fresh thyme
Coarse salt and freshly ground black pepper

FOR THE MUSHROOM STUFFING
1 tablespoon extra-virgin olive oil
2 tablespoons finely diced yellow onion
2 garlic cloves, finely minced
2 tablespoons finely diced fennel (reserve the fronds from the stalks)
2 cups thinly sliced fresh shiitake mushroom caps
¼ cup very thinly sliced napa cabbage
2 tablespoons grated celery root
8 fresh chervil leaves, roughly torn
Coarse salt and freshly ground black pepper

shiitake chips | Preheat the oven to 300°F.

Place the shiitake mushroom caps, rounded side up, on a parchment-paper-lined rimmed baking sheet. Cover the mushrooms with another piece of parchment, and then place another baking sheet on top of the mushrooms. Bake until the mushrooms are dried out and crisp, about 2½ hours. Remove from the oven, lift off the top baking sheet, and set aside to cool completely on the baking sheet. Then peel the mushrooms off the paper and place them in an airtight container.

morels | Place the morels in a medium bowl, and add hot water to cover by 2 inches. Cover the bowl with plastic wrap and set it aside for 20 minutes. Drain the morels and set them aside.

In a medium skillet, melt the butter over medium heat. Add the leek and cook, stirring often, until soft, about 4 minutes. Stir in the garlic and cook until it is fragrant, about 1 minute, and then pour in the port, scraping up any browned bits from the bottom of the pan. Add the morels, cook for 1 minute to warm them through, and then stir in the thyme and some salt and pepper. Turn off the heat and set aside.

mushroom stuffing | In a large skillet, heat the olive oil over medium-low heat. Add the onion and garlic and cook, stirring often, for 2 minutes, until they're translucent. Stir in the fennel and the sliced shiitakes, and cook until soft, 3 to 4 minutes. Mix in the cabbage, cook 1 minute longer, and then remove from the heat. Stir in the celery root and chervil, and season the mixture with salt and pepper.

serve | Place the shiitake chips, bottom side up, on a platter, and place 1 teaspoon of the mushroom stuffing on each chip. Top with a morel, and serve.

MAKE AHEAD The shiitake chips can be stored in an airtight container at room temperature for up to 5 days.

The mushroom stuffing can be made 1 day before serving; cover and refrigerate.

> **TIP** For extra flavor, soak 1 ounce of dried morels in warm water for 20 minutes. Drain, chop, and sauté them with the shiitakes for the stuffing.

mini challah loaves

MAKES 8 LOAVES

Rather than making full-sized dinner rolls or bread sticks, I make these adorable mini braided challah loaves. Their shape, size, and glossy brown crust make them an arresting bread course whether served with butter, pâté, or on their own. I like to serve them in a tiny bread basket or on a small cutting board.

½ cup warm (100° to 105°F.) water
1½ tablespoons honey
1½ teaspoons active dry yeast
1 large egg
3 large egg yolks
1 tablespoon plus 2 teaspoons vegetable oil
1 teaspoon coarse salt
2½ cups bread flour, plus extra for kneading

In the bowl of a stand mixer, whisk together the water, honey, and yeast. Cover the bowl with plastic wrap and set it aside in a warm, draft-free spot until the mixture is foamy, about 5 minutes.

Remove the plastic wrap and whisk in the egg, 1 egg yolk, 1 tablespoon of the oil, and the salt. Add 1 cup of the flour, and using the paddle attachment, beat the mixture on low speed until the dough is very sticky and webby, 2 to 3 minutes. Turn off the mixer and let the dough rest for 15 minutes.

Add the remaining 1½ cups flour, and using the dough hook attachment, mix the dough on medium speed until the flour is completely incorporated and the dough forms a rough ball. Turn the dough out onto a lightly floured work surface, and knead it by hand until it is smooth and soft-textured yet forms a nice ball, 6 to 8 minutes. If the dough becomes too sticky to handle or doesn't form a ball, knead 1 tablespoon of flour at a time into the dough until it reaches the desired consistency.

Grease a bowl with the remaining 2 teaspoons of vegetable oil and place the dough ball in the bowl, turning it over to oil all sides of the ball. Cover the bowl with plastic wrap and set it aside in a warm, draft-free spot until the dough has doubled in size, about 1½ hours.

Punch down the dough and turn it out onto a lightly floured work surface. Break the dough into 24 pieces (about ½ ounce each) and roll them into 4-inch-long, ¼-inch-wide ropes. Connect 3 ropes at one end and loosely braid the ropes. Pinch the dough at the other end so the braid doesn't unravel, and place the shaped loaf on a parchment-paper-lined baking sheet. Repeat with the remaining pieces of dough to make 8 loaves. Cover the baking sheet loosely with plastic wrap and set it aside until the loaves have doubled in size, about 20 minutes.

Meanwhile, preheat the oven to 375°F.

In a small bowl, whisk the remaining 2 egg yolks with 1 tablespoon water to make an egg wash. Remove the plastic wrap from the baking sheet and lightly brush each loaf with egg wash. Bake the challah for 10 minutes. Reduce the heat to 350°F. and continue to bake until the loaves are golden brown, about 8 minutes longer. Remove the bread from the oven and set aside to cool.

Place the bread in linen-lined bread baskets or serve it on small cutting boards. The bread can be served slightly warm or completely cooled.

MAKE AHEAD The challah can be baked, cooled, and frozen for up to 3 weeks. Thaw at room temperature for 2 to 3 hours and then warm in a 350°F. oven for 2 to 3 minutes before serving.

lobster-potato petit fours

MAKES 2 DOZEN

My wife, Josephine Sasso, is a dress designer. She loves petit fours, so one day I thought of making a savory petit four and created this hors d'oeuvre especially for her. With its coral palette, the lobster is presented as a square-cut jewel in a perfect potato setting. If you prefer, cooked shrimp can be substituted for the lobster.

FOR THE POTATO PETIT FOURS
3 large Yukon Gold potatoes
6 cups peanut oil
2 teaspoons coarse salt

FOR THE LOBSTER
1 ripe avocado, halved and pitted
1 tablespoon fresh lemon juice
Coarse salt
1½ cups diced cooked lobster meat
1 tablespoon mayonnaise
2 tablespoons store-bought pesto

potato petit fours | Slice the potatoes crosswise into ½-inch-thick rounds. Use a ½-inch square cookie cutter to stamp out squares from each potato slice (you want 24 total; if you don't have a square-shaped cutter, you can use a round one). Use a small melon baller to scoop out a small portion of the center of each square, making a cuplike indentation. Take care not to puncture the sides or the bottom of the square.

In a large pot, heat the oil to 375°F. over medium heat. Add the potatoes (you don't want to overcrowd the pot, so you may need to fry them in batches) and fry until golden brown, turning them often so they brown on all sides, 1½ to 2 minutes. Use a slotted spoon or a frying spider to transfer the crispy potatoes to a paper-towel-lined plate. Sprinkle with the salt. Set aside to cool completely.

lobster | Scoop the avocado into the bowl of a food processor. Add the lemon juice and ¼ teaspoon salt, and process until smooth. Transfer to a squeeze bottle.

serve | In a small bowl, stir together the lobster, mayonnaise, and a pinch of salt. Place ¼ teaspoon of the pesto in the center of each potato. Top with the lobster mixture, and finish with a dot of avocado purée.

MAKE AHEAD The potato squares can be fried several hours ahead and set aside at room temperature.

The avocado purée can be made and covered with plastic wrap and refrigerated up to 2 hours before serving.

salmon tarts

MAKES 2 DOZEN

This hors d'oeuvre is stunning: diced smoked salmon brightened by a briny caper in a cup of crisp salmon skin. The cups are a light and crunchy variation on the traditional baked butter-and-flour tart crust. I am reminded how often a minimal, natural approach looks best. For the best salmon skin, go to a good fish store or fish counter and ask for it—they'll often give it to you for free. See page 250 for sources of smoked sea salt.

FOR THE SALMON SKIN CUPS

2 pounds salmon skin
Coarse salt and freshly ground black pepper

FOR THE SALMON TOPPING

3 cups vegetable oil
½ cup brine-packed capers, drained, rinsed, and placed on a kitchen towel to dry
8 ounces smoked salmon, sliced lengthwise into ¼-inch-wide strips and then crosswise into ¼-inch pieces
1 tablespoon extra-virgin olive oil
1 teaspoon grated lemon zest
¼ teaspoon smoked sea salt

salmon skin cups | Preheat the oven to 350°F.

Lay the salmon skin flat on a baking sheet, scale side down. Sprinkle with some salt and pepper, and bake until some of the fat renders off, 17 to 20 minutes. Remove the salmon skin from the oven and set it aside to cool completely, about 1 hour.

Once the salmon skin is cool, use a 2-inch square cookie cutter (or a chef's knife) to cut out 24 squares.

Place each salmon skin square in a cup of a 24-cup mini muffin pan, fitting it in so the edges just reach the top to form a cup shape. Fit a second mini muffin pan over the salmon skins, pressing the pan down slightly. Bake until the salmon skins are crisp, about 8 minutes. Remove the pans from the oven, lift off the second muffin tin, and set aside to cool completely, about 30 minutes. Then remove the salmon skin cups from the pan.

salmon topping | In a medium saucepan, heat the vegetable oil to 375°F. over medium heat. Add the capers and fry until crisp, about 1 minute. Remove the capers, using a fine-mesh skimmer or a frying spider, and place them on a paper-towel-lined plate to drain. Set aside.

In a medium bowl, gently toss the diced salmon with the olive oil, lemon zest, and smoked salt.

serve | Place the salmon cups on a serving platter and mound the chopped salmon in them. Finish with a fried caper, and serve.

pheasant under glass

MAKES 2 DOZEN

The legendary pheasant under glass harks back to an era of fine dining when domed platters, polished silver, and white-gloved waiters symbolized the epitome of luxury. I loved the idea of re-creating it, so we miniaturized the dish and asked a glass studio to hand-blow tiny glass domes for us. (Crate & Barrel and Pottery Barn often have small glass domes with matching platters in stock; see page 250.) At parties, waiters pass the tray and pause when they lift the dome to announce, "Pheasant under glass!" It's a little campy but it's fun, and guests love it. The dish can be made with chicken breasts instead of pheasant: Follow the recipe below, marinating the meat for a maximum of 3 hours.

FOR THE PHEASANT
½ cup port wine
¼ cup raspberry vinegar
2 tablespoons walnut oil
1 large shallot, finely minced
¼ cup roughly chopped fresh basil leaves
1 2-inch piece fresh ginger, peeled and sliced into thin rounds
1½ teaspoons ground coriander
1½ teaspoons freshly ground black pepper
2 6-ounce boneless skin-on pheasant breasts
Coarse salt and freshly ground black pepper
2 tablespoons vegetable oil
¼ cup Asian plum sauce

FOR THE POTATO NESTS
5 large russet potatoes, cut into 24 ¼-inch-thick rounds
2 tablespoons extra-virgin olive oil
Coarse salt

FOR THE PLUM JAM
2 tablespoons Asian plum sauce
½ teaspoon ground coriander
¼ teaspoon minced peeled fresh ginger

FOR SERVING
1 Granny Smith apple
1 teaspoon fresh lemon juice
72 thawed, frozen edamame beans (about ¼ cup)

pheasant | Place the port, raspberry vinegar, walnut oil, shallot, basil, ginger, coriander, and pepper in a gallon-sized resealable food storage bag, seal it shut, and shake to combine. Add the pheasant breasts, seal, turn to coat in the marinade, and refrigerate for at least 3 hours or overnight.

Preheat the oven to 350°F.

Remove the breasts from the marinade and season them with salt and pepper. In a medium ovenproof skillet, heat the vegetable oil over medium-high heat. Add the breasts, skin side down, and cook until golden brown, 5 to 8 minutes. Turn them over and brown the other side, 4 to 5 minutes. Turn off the heat and brush the pheasant with the plum sauce. Bake in the oven until cooked through, 5 to 8 minutes. Remove from the oven and allow to cool. Then cut into ½-inch cubes.

potato nests | Use a 1½-inch round cookie cutter to cut out a round from each potato slice. Set 1 round on a cutting board. Using a paring knife, slice horizontally halfway through the potato, leaving the knife in the center of the potato (you'll have split potato on one side and solid potato on the other). Place a 1-inch round cookie cutter over the center of the potato and press down until you hit the blade of the knife (this prevents the cutter from slicing all the way through). Remove the cutter and the cut-out 1-inch round, forming a cup in the center of the potato slice. Place the potato on a parchment-paper-lined rimmed baking sheet. Repeat with the remaining potato slices.

Season the potatoes with the olive oil and salt to taste, and roast at 350°F. until golden brown and crispy, about 25 minutes.

plum jam | In a small bowl, whisk the plum sauce, coriander, and ginger together. Set aside.

serve | Peel, core, and slice the apple into
⅛-inch-thick pieces. Cut the pieces into twenty-
four ¼-inch triangles, and sprinkle with the
lemon juice to delay browning.

Place 3 edamame beans in each potato nest.
Top with ¼ teaspoon of the plum jam and a
pheasant cube. Finish with a triangle of green
apple. Serve under a glass dome.

MAKE AHEAD The plum jam can be refrigerated for up to
1 week.

The pheasant can be refrigerated for up to 1 day before
serving.

The potato nests can be set aside at room temperature
for up to a few hours before serving.

TIP Instead of using lemon juice to prevent the
apples from browning, you can submerge them
in a small bowl of lemon-lime soda!

TIP For the same presentation in half the time, buy prepared pigs in blankets and serve them with the pigs in a field.

pigs in blankets, two ways

MAKES 2 DOZEN OF EACH

Here it is, the number one most-requested hors d'oeuvre at parties: pigs in puff pastry blankets. As a caterer who takes pride in imprinting dishes with my distinct spin, I was thrilled to remake this party workhorse. My rendition is smoked salmon "pigs" with wasabi caviar "blankets" perched above a field of living wheatgrass. I love how the *New York Times* described it in a feature: "This little pig went, well, a little crazy." I like to serve it with the classic version to satisfy the traditionalists. We have also cut the salmon and bread with an Oscar-shaped cutter for Academy Awards parties. If you can't find wasabi caviar (see Resources, page 250), substitute very finely chopped fresh dill.

FOR THE CLASSIC PIGS IN BLANKETS
1 12-ounce package all-beef cocktail franks
1 sheet frozen puff pastry, thawed
1 large egg
2 tablespoons Dijon mustard

FOR THE PIGS IN A FIELD
4 tablespoons (½ stick) unsalted butter, at room temperature
1 teaspoon brine-packed capers, drained and finely chopped
1 tablespoon grated lemon zest
12 slices pumpernickel bread
12 ounces sliced smoked salmon, such as lox
24 black sesame seeds
2 ounces wasabi caviar (or 2 tablespoons finely chopped fresh dill)

pigs in blankets | Remove the cocktail franks from the package and place them on a paper-towel-lined plate to absorb any extra moisture. Place the puff pastry on a cutting board and slice it into twenty-four 2-inch-long, ¾-inch-wide strips. Place a frank horizontally in the center of a strip. Bring the edges of the pastry over the frank, pinch together, and set the pastry, seam side down, on a parchment-paper-lined rimmed baking sheet. Repeat with the remaining franks and puff strips, placing the pigs in blankets about 1 inch apart. Place the baking sheet in the freezer and chill for 20 minutes.

Preheat the oven to 350°F.

In a small bowl, whisk 1 tablespoon water with the egg to make an egg wash. Remove the baking sheet from the freezer and brush the egg wash over the pastry. Bake, rotating the pan midway through, until the pastry is golden brown, about 24 minutes. Set aside to cool.

pigs in a field | In a small bowl, stir the butter, capers, and lemon zest together. Set aside.

Using a 2-inch pig-shaped cookie cutter, cut the bread and the salmon into 24 bread pig shapes and 24 salmon pig shapes. Spread one side of each piece of bread with ¼ teaspoon of the lemon-caper butter. Carefully lay a piece of pig-shaped smoked salmon over the buttered bread. Place a sesame seed where the eye should be. Make a stripe of caviar down the middle of each pig's belly (see photo, opposite) with ¼ teaspoon of the wasabi caviar.

serve | Serve the traditional pigs in blankets with a dot of mustard on each. Serve the pigs in a field standing in a tray of wheatgrass (or print a picture of grass and place it beneath a piece of glass or clear acrylic and serve the salmon-wasabi pigs on top).

MAKE AHEAD Traditional pigs in blankets can be kept frozen for 1 month.

The lemon-caper butter can be made 1 week ahead; cover and refrigerate.

The smoked salmon-wasabi pigs can be assembled and refrigerated for several hours before serving.

potted shrimp

MAKES 2 DOZEN

Potted shrimp, a kind of shrimp porridge made with lots of butter, has a very staid, buttoned-up English pedigree (it was a favorite of author Ian Fleming as well as his most famous character, James Bond). I turn it on its head by taking it quite literally and serving shrimp in pastry pots with pretty edible flowers poking through.

FOR THE POTS
1½ cups all-purpose flour
2 tablespoons sweet paprika
6 tablespoons (⅔ stick) unsalted butter, cut into small pieces
1½ tablespoons solid vegetable shortening
Nonstick pan spray
1½ cups dried beans

FOR THE SHRIMP
24 medium shrimp (41–50 count per pound), cooked, peeled, deveined, and tails removed
2 tablespoons extra-virgin olive oil
1 tablespoon finely chopped fresh chives
Grated zest of 1 lemon
¼ teaspoon coarse salt
24 fresh micro green sprigs (or edible flowers)

pots | Using a food processor, pulse the flour and paprika together. Add the butter and shortening, and pulse until the mixture is sandy. With the motor running, add 3 tablespoons water, stopping the processor just when the dry ingredients come together. Transfer the dough to a piece of plastic wrap, flatten it into a disk, wrap, and refrigerate for 1 hour.

Preheat the oven to 350°F. Lightly coat twenty-four 1-inch terra-cotta flowerpots with nonstick pan spray.

Unwrap the dough and place it between two sheets of parchment paper. Roll until it is $\frac{1}{16}$-inch thick. Remove the top layer of parchment and slice the dough into twenty-four 2½-inch-long, 1-inch-wide strips. Use the scraps to make 24 small balls of dough, each about the size of a pea. Place 1 strip in each pot so it runs around the sides of the pot, and use your fingers to press the dough flat around the edges. Drop a small ball of dough inside the pot and press down to make the bottom. Fill each pot with 1 tablespoon of the dried beans, and place the pots on a rimmed baking sheet. Bake until the dough is set, about 25 minutes. Remove the pots from the oven and let them cool completely. Then remove the beans and carefully tap each pot to release the pastry.

shrimp | In a medium bowl, toss the cooked shrimp with the olive oil, chives, lemon zest, and salt.

serve | Divide the shrimp among the pots, and finish each one with some micro greens or an edible flower.

MAKE AHEAD The pots can be made 1 day ahead and stored in an airtight container at room temperature.

The shrimp can be seasoned and refrigerated for up to 2 hours before serving.

> **TIP** Skip making the pastry pots and serve the shrimp right in clean 1-inch flowerpots.

deviled quail eggs

MAKES 2 DOZEN

Deviled eggs are an old-hat hors d'oeuvre that was just begging to be made over. I married the idea to speckled quail eggs. Standing them upright makes them more elegant than their picnic-lunch counterpart, as does serving them with a row of beautiful unshelled quail's eggs down the center of the tray. Just be sure that the eggs are hard-boiled—people *will* grab them and crack them, assuming that they are! If you can't find quail eggs, you can make these with medium chicken eggs; see the Variation below.

FOR THE EGG CUPS
24 quail eggs

FOR THE DEVILED FILLING
3 hard-boiled egg yolks (from chicken eggs), mashed
1 tablespoon mayonnaise
1 teaspoon Dijon mustard
A few drops of Tabasco sauce
1 teaspoon coarse salt
⅛ teaspoon finely ground white pepper

FOR SERVING
24 fresh dill fronds

egg cups | Prepare an ice water bath and place it next to your work surface. Place the quail eggs in a medium pot and add cold water to cover by 2 inches. Cover the pan and bring to a boil, swirling the pan a few times as the water heats up (this helps the yolks stay centered in the eggs). As soon as the water comes to a boil, remove the cover and reduce the heat to medium-low. Simmer gently for 2 minutes, and turn off the heat. Use a slotted spoon to transfer the eggs to the ice water bath, and let them cool for 5 minutes.

Remove the eggs from the ice water and dry them off; then gently roll them on a hard surface to crack the shells. Peel off the shells, slice off the top third of each egg, carefully remove the yolks, and place them in a medium bowl (save the top third of the eggs for serving). Use a fork to mash the yolks, and set aside.

deviled filling | Add the chicken yolks, mayonnaise, mustard, Tabasco, salt, and pepper to the mashed quail egg yolks. Mix until well combined. Scrape the mixture into a pastry bag fitted with a small star tip.

serve | Place the eggs on a platter and pipe some of the deviled filling into each one. Place the top portion of the egg back on top, top with a dill frond, and serve.

MAKE AHEAD The quail eggs can be hard-boiled 1 day ahead and refrigerated.

The deviled filling can be made 1 day ahead. Cover it directly with plastic wrap to prevent it from drying out and refrigerate.

The filled eggs can be prepared, then covered with plastic wrap, and refrigerated several hours before serving.

TIP Because they're so small, removing the hard-boiled yolks from the quail eggs can be tricky. Save time by leaving the yolks in the quail eggs and using 8 hard-boiled large egg yolks in place of the quail egg yolks to make the deviled filling. Pipe the filling right on top of the trimmed quail eggs and garnish as described.

VARIATION

If you can't find quail eggs, you can make this with medium chicken eggs. Halve the peeled hard-boiled eggs and pop out the yolks. Save 8 yolks to make the filling as described in the recipe.

vegetable spring rolls

MAKES 2 DOZEN

Vietnamese spring rolls (sometimes called summer rolls) are wonderfully light and fresh. This recipe is pretty true to the original version—it's our vertical presentation on cucumber holders that sets them apart.

FOR THE PICKLED CABBAGE
3 tablespoons fresh lime juice
1 tablespoon (packed) light brown sugar
1 teaspoon fish sauce
¼ teaspoon Sriracha hot sauce
¼ cup thinly sliced napa cabbage

FOR THE SPRING ROLLS
½ seedless (English) cucumber, peeled
½ red bell pepper
1 large carrot
12 fresh snow peas
2 tablespoons toasted sesame oil
48 fresh shiitake mushrooms, stems removed, caps thinly sliced
Coarse salt and freshly ground black pepper
24 8½-inch rice papers
24 large fresh basil leaves
48 fresh mint leaves
24 pickled ginger slices
24 fresh cilantro sprigs with 3 to 4 leaves on each sprig

FOR THE CUCUMBER HOLDERS
2 seedless (English) cucumbers

pickled cabbage | In a medium bowl, whisk the lime juice, brown sugar, fish sauce, and Sriracha together. Stir the cabbage into the sauce, and set aside for 5 minutes. Then drain the cabbage.

spring rolls | Slice the cucumber into ¼-inch-thick, ⅛-inch-wide strips, and set aside. Slice the bell pepper, carrot, and snow peas into 2-inch-long, ⅛-inch-wide strips, and set aside.

Heat the sesame oil in a large skillet over medium-high heat. Add the mushrooms and cook until they just begin to become tender, about 2 minutes. Season with salt and pepper, turn off the heat, and turn the mushrooms out onto a plate to cool.

One at a time, place all the rice papers in a large bowl of warm water. Let the rice papers soak until they're pliable, 5 to 10 minutes.

Remove a rice paper from the water and place it on a cutting board. Starting 1 inch from the bottom, place a basil leaf, 2 mint leaves, 2 cucumber slices, 2 bell pepper slices, 2 carrot strips, 2 slices of snow pea, ½ tablespoon pickled cabbage, 1½ tablespoons mushrooms, 2 slices pickled ginger, and a cilantro sprig. Roll the bottom inch of the wrapper up and over the filling, and then tuck it in to form a tight cylinder. Keep rolling until you reach the middle, then tuck in the ends and continue to roll to seal the spring roll. Place it on a plate. Repeat with the remaining rice papers and filling ingredients. Refrigerate, covered with plastic wrap, until serving.

cucumber holders | Slice the cucumbers in half lengthwise, and then in half crosswise so you have a total of 8 pieces. Slice a thin strip lengthwise off the top and bottom of each cucumber segment. Make a lengthwise slit through the

(recipe continues)

middle of 1 cucumber, almost all the way to the end. Leave the knife in the cucumber (it acts as a barrier so you won't slice all the way through when you make the cups for the spring rolls). Use a round 1-inch cookie cutter to stamp three rounds out of the top of the cucumber (when the cutter hits the knife, you know you've gone deep enough). Remove the cucumber rounds. The remaining cups will act as holders for the spring rolls. Repeat with the remaining cucumber segments.

serve | Remove the spring rolls from the refrigerator. Slice each one in half on the diagonal, and stand it, open end up, in a cucumber holder. Serve.

MAKE AHEAD The pickled cabbage and the vegetables can be prepared 1 day ahead; cover and refrigerate.

The spring rolls can be prepared and refrigerated on a plate, covered with plastic wrap, for up to 4 hours before serving.

VARIATION

mango, shrimp, avocado spring rolls

Julienne the ingredients and roll, as done with the Vegetable Spring Rolls. Use pickled ginger, herbs, and sauce, as in the Vegetable Spring Rolls.

blts

MAKES 2 DOZEN

For this bread-free light bite I combine one of my favorite lunches, the BLT, with the summery look of on-the-vine tomatoes. The tomatoes, especially if you can find them in vibrant yellows, oranges, and reds, make great holders for the bacon and avocado-topped cherry tomatoes. These are delicious without the bacon, too—I like to substitute a hard, somewhat salty slice of cheese, like Pecorino.

12 large cherry tomatoes, cut into wedges
1 avocado
1 tablespoon fresh lemon juice
Coarse salt
24 medium yellow tomatoes
2 ruffled green lettuce leaves, torn into 24 pieces
1 tablespoon mayonnaise
3 bacon strips, cooked until crisp and then sliced into
    ¼- to ½-inch pieces

Use a small melon baller to scoop the seeds out from each cherry tomato wedge. Discard the seeds and set the tomato wedges aside.

Halve the avocado, remove the pit, peel away the skin, and chop the avocado into ¼-inch cubes. Place them in a small bowl, sprinkle with the lemon juice and some salt, toss gently, and set aside.

Set the yellow tomatoes on a cutting board. Slice a small piece of tomato off one side of each one so it can balance without wobbling; then cut a small slice off the top (this is where the BLT will be placed). Place a piece of lettuce on top of the tomato.

Set the cherry tomato wedges on a tray and give each a small dot of mayonnaise. Top with several avocado cubes, and finish with a bit of bacon. Place the BLTs on top of the yellow tomatoes, and serve.

MAKE AHEAD The bacon can be cooked and refrigerated the day before serving.

The tomato wedges can be made and refrigerated in an airtight container up to 1 day in advance.

turkey canapés with stuffing and cranberry relish

MAKES 2 DOZEN

I tend to overindulge at Thanksgiving. I'm sure my sisters used to think that it was my way of getting out of doing the dishes! After one such holiday, I thought, Wouldn't it be great to serve all the classic dishes in miniature, saving me the pain from an overloaded plate? This is an hors d'oeuvre that comes with all the Turkey Day trimmings.

FOR THE TURKEY
2 tablespoons extra-virgin olive oil
1 tablespoon finely chopped fresh sage leaves
2 teaspoons finely chopped fresh thyme leaves
½ teaspoon coarse salt
¼ teaspoon freshly ground black pepper
1 4-pound skin-on boneless turkey breast

FOR THE STUFFING
½ loaf day-old peasant bread, cut into ½-inch cubes (2 cups)
¼ teaspoon dried sage leaves
¼ teaspoon coarse salt
⅛ teaspoon freshly ground black pepper
4 tablespoons (½ stick) unsalted butter
½ small yellow onion, finely chopped
½ medium carrot, finely chopped
½ celery stalk, finely chopped

FOR THE CRANBERRY SAUCE
1½ cups fresh or frozen cranberries
1 cup sugar
Grated zest and juice of 1 orange

FOR THE TURKEY SKIN CUPS
6 cups vegetable oil

turkey | Preheat the oven to 325°F.

Pour the olive oil into a small bowl and stir in the sage, thyme, salt, and pepper. Place the turkey breast, skin side up, on an aluminum-foil-lined rimmed baking sheet, and use your fingers to separate most of the skin from the meat, keeping one end still attached to create a pocket. Rub the herbed oil under the skin onto the breast. Roast the turkey until its internal temperature reads 165°F. on an instant-read thermometer, 45 minutes to 1 hour. (If the skin gets too dark, loosely tent the turkey breast with a sheet of foil.) Remove the turkey from the oven and set it aside to cool slightly, 10 minutes.

Raise the oven temperature to 375°F.

Peel off the turkey skin, trying to keep it in one piece. Use a 2-inch round cookie cutter to stamp out rounds of turkey skin. Place each round in a cup of a 24-cup mini muffin tin, and place a second mini muffin tin on top. Weight down the second tin with a few bricks or a small pot of water. Bake for 10 minutes. Remove from the oven and let cool for 10 minutes before removing the skins from the cups. They should be crispy.

Place the turkey meat on a cutting board and cut it into ¼-inch cubes. Set aside.

stuffing | Place the bread cubes, sage, salt, and pepper in a large bowl and set aside. In a large skillet over medium heat, melt 2 tablespoons of the butter. Pour it over the bread cubes, stirring to evenly coat them with butter and herbs. Transfer the seasoned bread cubes to an aluminum-foil-lined rimmed baking sheet, and toast in the oven until golden brown, 7 to 10 minutes. Let the bread cool for 10 minutes, and then turn it out into a bowl.

In the same skillet, melt the remaining

2 tablespoons butter over medium heat. Add the onion, carrot, and celery and cook, stirring often, until the vegetables are soft, 3 to 4 minutes. Add the vegetables to the seasoned bread cubes, and toss to combine.

cranberry sauce | In a small saucepan, stir the cranberries, sugar, and orange zest and juice together. Bring to a simmer over medium heat. Cook, stirring occasionally, until the liquid thickens and the cranberries begin to burst, 10 to 15 minutes. Transfer to a medium bowl and set aside to cool.

serve | Place the turkey skin cups on a platter. Divide the chopped turkey among the cups. Add a few cubes of the stuffing, and finish with a dollop of the cranberry sauce.

MAKE AHEAD The turkey breast can be roasted and then stored in an airtight container in the refrigerator for up to 1 day.

The turkey skin cups can be refrigerated in an airtight container for up to 1 day before serving. Let them sit at room temperature for at least 15 minutes before filling and serving.

The cranberry sauce can be refrigerated in an airtight container for up to 1 week.

MINIS GO MAIN

Spaghetti and Meatballs with Caesar Salad and Garlic Bread
Croque Monsieurs | Short Rib Burgers with Onion Rings
BBQ Chicken | Spicy Beef "Fortune Cookies"
Truffle Risotto Lollipops | Pea Soup and Caprese Salad
Lobster Under Glass

I AM OFTEN ASKED WHAT I DO FOR A MORE TRADITIONAL sit-down dinner that mimics the fanciful quality of my hors d'oeuvres. Since hors d'oeuvres are often everyone's favorite part of the meal, why not make them the whole meal? In this chapter, you'll find thoughtfully composed dishes that are slightly larger than the average party-sized portion but that still show off the same whimsy and wit that have become my trademarks.

To add a bit of fun, we serve dishes like burgers and onion rings, and meatballs and garlic bread, in untraditional ways. Croque monsieur sandwiches are presented upright, and barbecued chicken is served in a field of wheatgrass. Each guest gets his or her own fun portion, which brings that "ta-da" element of my parties to the table.

Three of these not-so-minis served together make for a very satisfying experience; or if you're serving hors d'oeuvres first, pare it down to two dishes. For a more informal dinner, guests can share from the same plate set on a coffee table or an ottoman. Arranging food throughout the room encourages your guests to interact and share. It's a great way to mesh the social aspect of a cocktail party with the satiety of a sit-down meal.

spaghetti and meatballs with caesar salad and garlic bread

SERVES 6

This spaghetti-and-meatball presentation is perhaps our most popular main-course offering, probably because it is a composition that pleases just about anyone. The trio is really a complete meal in itself. We often serve it on red-and-white-checkered plates for the "red sauce restaurant" look.

FOR THE MEATBALLS
Double recipe meatball mixture (page 35), shaped into
    12 balls
½ cup canned or homemade beef broth

FOR THE SPAGHETTI
1 teaspoon coarse salt
8 ounces angel hair pasta
1 cup store-bought Alfredo sauce (or homemade pasta
    sauce, page 35)

FOR THE GARLIC BREAD
2 tablespoons unsalted butter, at room temperature
1 tablespoon extra-virgin olive oil
6 garlic cloves, finely minced
¼ teaspoon coarse salt
1 baguette

FOR THE SALAD
1 head romaine lettuce, chopped into ½-inch pieces
1 cup store-bought Caesar salad dressing
1 2-ounce wedge Parmigiano-Reggiano cheese, shaved
    with a vegetable peeler
½ cup small seasoned croutons (preferably seasoned
    with just salt and pepper)

meatballs | Preheat the oven to 350°F.

Place the meat balls on a rimmed baking sheet. Pour ¼ cup of the beef broth into the pan and cover with aluminum foil. Bake until the meatballs are cooked through, 12 to 15 minutes. Remove the pan from the oven, remove and discard the foil, and let the meatballs cool to room temperature. Slice a small bit off the top and the bottom of each meatball to create a flat surface. Transfer the meatballs to a clean rimmed baking sheet and set aside.

spaghetti | Bring a large pot of water to a boil. Add the salt and the pasta, and cook, following the package instructions, until the pasta is al dente. Drain.

In a small saucepan, heat the Alfredo sauce just until warm; remove from the heat.

Stick a fondue fork into the pile of pasta and twirl it to make a 6- or 8-strand nest. Dip the nest into the warm Alfredo sauce, and then carefully slide the pasta off the fork onto the top of a meatball. Repeat for the remaining meatballs. Reserve the remaining Alfredo sauce.

garlic bread | In a small bowl, stir the butter, olive oil, garlic, and salt together. Slice the ends off the baguette, and then cut the baguette into 6 pieces. Make two vertical slits just shy of all the way through in each baguette segment. Use a butter knife to spread the garlic mixture between the slices and on the cut ends of the bread. Wrap the baguette pieces in aluminum foil and place them on a baking sheet.

(recipe continues)

salad | Place the lettuce in a large bowl and toss with the dressing.

serve | Preheat the oven to 350°F.

Place the garlic bread in the oven and heat until it's toasted, 7 to 10 minutes. Pour the remaining ¼ cup beef broth into the baking sheet holding the meatballs. Cover with aluminum foil and cook until the meatballs and pasta are warmed through, 5 to 6 minutes.

Meanwhile, divide the salad among six small bowls. Garnish with the shaved Parmesan and the croutons, and place on a plate. Unwrap the baguettes and place on the plate.

Remove the baking sheet from the oven, and finish each pasta-topped meatball with a dollop of the Alfredo sauce. Transfer 2 to each plate, and serve.

MAKE AHEAD The meatballs can be shaped, frozen on a baking sheet, and then transferred to a gallon-sized resealable freezer bag and frozen for up to 3 months. To thaw, let them sit out at room temperature for about 1 hour; then cook as directed.

The meatballs can be cooked, cooled, and refrigerated up to 1 day before serving.

The garlic bread can be made 1 day ahead, wrapped in foil, and refrigerated. Toast before serving.

TIP Small dishes of extras like warm tomato sauce, chopped fresh basil, cloves of roasted garlic, and shaved Parmigiano-Reggiano give the standard spaghetti and meatballs a customized touch. Serve in individual small dishes or ramekins, or family-style in larger bowls.

croque monsieurs

SERVES 6 (3 SANDWICHES PER PERSON)

Melted nutty Gruyère cheese and thin slices of pro-sciutto are fused together in our butter-toasted croque monsieurs, the sophisticated cousin of the ever-popular grilled cheese sandwich. They are a little smaller than a regular-sized grilled cheese but bigger than our minis—three makes for a perfect serving. We once made them for a *House & Garden* magazine dinner in a North Carolina castle, which just goes to show that a casual bistro favorite can be welcome in the most elegant of spaces. Five-and-a-half-inch disposable mini loaf pans are available in most supermarkets, often packaged in sets of three or four. See also the Resources section (page 250).

FOR THE BREAD
Nonstick pan spray
2 tablespoons all-purpose flour
Double recipe Bun Dough (page 45), kneaded, risen, ready to be shaped

FOR THE CROQUE MONSIEURS
8 tablespoons (1 stick) unsalted butter
1 pound thinly sliced Gruyère cheese
8 ounces thinly sliced prosciutto

bread | Grease three 3¼ × 5¾-inch loaf pans with nonstick pan spray. Dust your work surface with the flour. Scrape the bread dough onto the work surface and divide it into 3 equal pieces. Roll each piece of dough into a log shape and fit it into a loaf pan (the dough should reach about halfway up the sides of the pan). Place the loaf pans side by side on a rimmed baking sheet, cover with a damp kitchen towel, and set aside in a warm, draft-free spot until they have nearly doubled in size, about 1 hour.

Preheat the oven to 350°F.

Remove the towel from the pans and loosely cover each pan with a sheet of aluminum foil. Bake the bread for 20 minutes. Then remove the foil and bake until the tops are golden brown, about 20 minutes longer. Let the loaves cool in the pans. Once completely cool, remove the loaves from the pans.

croque monsieurs | Slice the ends off each bread loaf, and then slice each loaf into 12 thin pieces. Melt the butter in the microwave in a microwave-safe dish. Use a pastry brush to brush melted butter over one side of each piece of bread. Place the bread slices, buttered side down, on a baking sheet.

Use a 2-inch square cookie cutter (or a paring knife) to trim the cheese slices so they fit on the bread slices. Place 1 slice of cheese on half of the bread slices. Top each with 2 pieces of prosciutto, 1 slice of cheese, and a slice of bread, buttered side up.

serve | Heat a large nonstick griddle or skillet over medium heat, or heat a nonstick electric griddle to 325°F. Toast the sandwiches on each side until they're golden brown and the cheese is melted, about 1 minute per side. Transfer 3 to a plate and serve, preferably arranged standing upright.

MAKE AHEAD The bread can be baked, cooled, wrapped in plastic wrap, and frozen for up to 2 weeks before using. Defrost at room temperature and then slice.

The sandwiches can be made 1 day in advance. Reheat them in a 350°F. oven until the cheese is remelted, 3 to 4 minutes, and serve.

short rib burgers with onion rings

SERVES 6 (1 BURGER PER PERSON)

Slowly braised with wine and herbs, shredded short ribs make for a divine spin on the traditional burger. Paired with onion rings, this is a comfort-food home run that becomes a welcome and unexpected surprise bite for any occasion.

FOR THE BURGERS

2 pounds boneless beef short ribs
Coarse salt and freshly ground black pepper
2 tablespoons vegetable oil
1 carrot, cut into ½-inch pieces
1 celery stalk, cut into ½-inch pieces
1 parsnip, cut into ½-inch pieces
1 yellow onion, cut into ½-inch pieces
2 tablespoons all-purpose flour
2 tablespoons tomato paste
2 cups red wine, such as Chianti or Merlot
1 cup canned or homemade beef broth
3 fresh thyme sprigs
1 bay leaf

FOR THE ONION RINGS

2 cups low-fat buttermilk
1 12-ounce bottle dark beer
4 sweet onions, such as Maui or Vidalia, cut into
   ¼-inch-thick rings
2 cups panko breadcrumbs
½ cup all-purpose flour
1 teaspoon chili powder
1 teaspoon coarse salt
½ teaspoon freshly ground black pepper

FOR SERVING

2 cups peanut oil
6 mini burger or slider buns (page 42), halved
Aioli (page 62)

burgers | Preheat the oven to 325°F.

Season the short ribs with salt and pepper. In a large heavy-bottomed ovenproof pot, heat the oil over medium-high heat. Add the short ribs and cook on both sides until browned, 2 to 3 minutes per side. Transfer the meat to a large bowl, and place the carrot, celery, parsnip, and onion in the pot. Cook, stirring often, until they start to soften, 5 to 7 minutes. Sprinkle the flour over the vegetables and cook for 1 minute longer. Stir in the tomato paste, and then pour in the wine and beef broth. Add the thyme sprigs and bay leaf, return the meat to the pot, cover, and bring to a simmer. Place the pot in the oven and cook until a fork easily shreds the meat, 2 to 2½ hours.

Remove the pot from the oven, uncover, and let the mixture cool. Remove and discard the bay leaf and thyme sprigs. Transfer the meat to a large bowl, and using your fingers or two forks, shred the meat. Pour the liquid and vegetables from the pot into a blender. Purée, taste for seasoning, and add salt and pepper if needed. Pour the sauce over the shredded meat and stir together so the meat gets nicely coated with sauce. Set aside.

onion rings | While the meat is cooking in the oven, marinate the onions: In a large bowl, whisk the buttermilk and beer together. Add the onion rings and set aside for 1 to 2 hours.

When you are ready to cook the onion rings, whisk together the panko, flour, chili powder, salt, and pepper in a large bowl. Drain the onion rings, reserving the buttermilk marinade. Dredge each onion ring through the panko mixture, dip it back in the buttermilk mixture, and then recoat it with the panko. Place on a rimmed baking sheet and repeat with the remaining onion rings.

serve │ Preheat the oven to 350°F. In a large pot, heat the peanut oil to 350°F. over medium heat.

Place about 3 tablespoons of the saucy meat on each bun. Place the burgers on a rimmed baking sheet, cover with aluminum foil, and warm in the oven for 4 to 5 minutes.

Meanwhile, fry the onion rings, a few at a time, in the hot oil until they're golden brown, using a slotted spoon or a frying spider to turn them as they cook, about 1 minute per side. Transfer the onion rings to a paper-towel-lined plate. Serve each burger alongside a few stacked onion rings and aioli (see page 62).

MAKE AHEAD The rolls can be baked, cooled, wrapped in plastic wrap, and frozen for up to 2 weeks before using. Thaw at room temperature and then halve.

The short ribs can be cooked and refrigerated in an airtight container for up to 1 day ahead of serving.

> **TIP** Use store-bought frozen onion rings instead of making your own.

bbq chicken

SERVES 6

Branding barbecued chicken with "BBQ" initials gives these lollipops a deep char-grilled flavor without having to light a grill. We serve the barbecue sauce on the side and use part of a tray of wheatgrass for presenting the chicken.

See page 250 for branding iron sources. You can also use B- and Q-shaped cookie cutters to cut out the chicken and skip the branding iron step.

2 tablespoons extra-virgin olive oil
1 teaspoon coarse salt
¼ teaspoon freshly ground black pepper
6 6-ounce boneless, skinless chicken breasts
Wooden skewers
¾ cup store-bought barbecue sauce

Preheat the oven to 350°F.

In a large bowl, whisk together the olive oil, salt, and pepper. Place the chicken on a large plate and rub both sides with the seasoned oil. Heat a cast-iron grill pan over high heat, and sear the chicken on both sides until it has grill marks, about 1 minute per side.

Heat "B" and "Q" branding irons according to the manufacturer's instructions, and brand each chicken breast with the BBQ initials. Use a round cookie cutter (with a diameter slightly larger than the branded letter) to cut the letters out from the chicken breast.

Place the branded chicken rounds in a 9 × 11-inch baking dish, and bake them in the oven until cooked through, 7 to 10 minutes.

Insert a skewer into each chicken round. Stick them in a tray of wheatgrass, or serve on a platter, with the barbecue sauce in a small dish on the side.

Branded! | Branding irons are a great way to add a personal touch to small bites. Purchase the branding irons in the initials of the guest of honor or to spell a short word (like BBQ or BOY or GIRL for a baby shower). Here are other foods in addition to the chicken that can be easily branded.
- Grilled Cheese (page 53)
- Lamb Lollipops (page 95)
- Baked Potatoes (page 30)
- French Toast (page 165)
- Burger Buns (page 45)

spicy beef "fortune cookies"

SERVES 4 (3 FORTUNE COOKIES PER PERSON)

Fortune cookies served as a savory dish are one of our biggest hits, and it is really fun to serve them as a main course in a Chinese restaurant take-out box (see Resources, page 250). To customize the boxes for your events, you can monogram them with the host's initials or the date of the party. Don't forget to make fortunes to tuck into the cookies. We like to include trivia questions that circle back to the guests—such as favorite hobbies—with the answers on the back.

1 pound 80% lean ground beef
3 scallions, white and green parts, finely minced
6 garlic cloves, finely minced
2 tablespoons brown miso paste
1 tablespoon soy sauce
1 1-inch piece fresh ginger, peeled and grated
¼ teaspoon cayenne pepper
Coarse salt and freshly ground black pepper
2 tablespoons all-purpose flour
1 package 8-inch spring roll wrappers
6 cups peanut oil
12 paper strips with fortunes

In a large bowl, mix together the ground beef, scallions, garlic, miso, soy sauce, ginger, cayenne, and some salt and black pepper. In a small bowl, whisk the flour with 3 tablespoons water, and set aside.

Lay the spring roll wrappers out on your work surface. Use a 4-inch round cookie cutter to cut 12 rounds from the wrappers. Place 9 of the rounds on a baking sheet, and cover them with a damp kitchen towel. Place 1½ tablespoons of the beef mixture just below the center of each of the 3 rounds remaining on the work surface. Dip your finger into the flour paste and moisten the outer edge of each wrapper. Fold the top over and press the edges together to seal, making a half-moon shape. Bend the tips of the half-moon together so they meet to make a fortune cookie shape. Transfer to a baking sheet, and repeat with the remaining filling and wrappers.

In a large pot, heat the oil to 350°F. over medium heat. Fry the fortune cookies, a few at a time, turning them often with a slotted spoon or a frying spider, until they're golden brown and cooked all the way through, 3 to 4 minutes. (If they brown too quickly, reduce the heat; if they take too long to brown, increase the heat.) As they are done, transfer the fortune cookies to a paper-towel-lined baking sheet to drain. Insert a paper fortune into each one, and serve.

MAKE AHEAD The fortune cookies can be filled and shape up to 2 weeks ahead, and then frozen. Thaw overnight in the refrigerator, and fry before serving.

truffle risotto lollipops

SERVES 6 (3 LOLLIPOPS PER PERSON)

For a swank spin on risotto, make these truffled lollipops for your next dinner party. Everyone always thinks that black truffles are so expensive, but they are a lot cheaper than a steak dinner for six!

2½ tablespoons extra-virgin olive oil
1 small yellow onion, finely chopped
1¼ cups arborio rice
2 garlic cloves, finely minced
½ teaspoon coarse salt
⅛ teaspoon freshly ground black pepper
⅓ cup dry white wine, such as Sauvignon Blanc
3 cups vegetable or chicken broth, warmed
¼ cup finely grated Parmigiano-Reggiano cheese
½ tablespoon white truffle oil
½ ounce fresh or jarred black truffles (see Resources, page 250)
18 lollipop sticks

In a large heavy-bottomed pot, heat the olive oil over medium-high heat. Reduce the heat to medium, add the onion, and cook, stirring often, until soft, about 5 minutes. Stir in the rice and the garlic and cook, stirring, until the rice is evenly coated with the oil.

Add the salt, pepper, and wine, and cook until the wine has evaporated. Reduce the heat to medium-low and pour in enough broth to just cover the rice; then stir until the broth is absorbed.

Continue to add more broth, ½ cup at a time, stirring after each addition until the broth is absorbed, the rice is cooked through (it should still be al dente in the center, like pasta), and the risotto is creamy, about 30 minutes total.

Stir in the Parmesan cheese and the truffle oil, and remove from the heat. Taste for seasoning and adjust if necessary. Line a rimmed 9 × 12-inch baking sheet with parchment paper, and use a rubber spatula to scrape the risotto onto the baking sheet. Spread the risotto so it is just under ½-inch thick. Cover with plastic wrap and refrigerate overnight.

The following day, uncover the risotto and use a 2-inch round cookie cutter to cut out 18 cakes for the lollipops.

Shave the black truffle and place 1 piece in the center of each risotto cake. If serving at room temperature, place the lollipop sticks in the cakes and serve. If serving warm, then cover the risotto cakes with a sheet of aluminum foil, heat them in a 350°F. oven for 2 to 3 minutes, insert the lollipop sticks, and serve.

MAKE AHEAD The risotto can be made up to 2 days before serving.

pea soup and caprese salad

SERVES 6

I like combining what are traditionally considered two separate courses onto one plate. Fresh pea soup with a hint of tarragon and refreshing caprese salad complement each other nicely. Pairing them cuts down on the fuss and time of serving them as individual soup and salad courses. This combo is my favorite way to begin a light spring or summer meal.

FOR THE PEA SOUP
1 tablespoon unsalted butter
1 medium leek, white part only, finely chopped
½ small yellow onion, finely chopped
1 garlic clove
1½ cups vegetable or chicken broth
1 bay leaf
¼ teaspoon coarse salt
Pinch of freshly ground black pepper
8 ounces fresh or semi-thawed frozen green peas
1 tablespoon finely chopped fresh tarragon

FOR THE CAPRESE SALAD
6 red cherry or grape tomatoes, quartered
6 yellow cherry or grape tomatoes, quartered
2 ounces fresh mozzarella cheese, sliced ½-inch thick
    and cut into ½-inch cubes
2 tablespoons extra-virgin olive oil
¼ teaspoon coarse salt
Pinch of freshly ground black pepper
12 medium to large unblemished basil leaves, plus
    12 small basil sprigs for garnish (optional)

pea soup | In a medium pot, melt the butter over medium heat. Add the leek and cook until soft, stirring often, about 10 minutes. Add the onion and cook until soft (if it starts browning, reduce the heat to medium-low), 3 to 4 minutes. Then stir in the garlic and cook until it's fragrant, 30 seconds to 1 minute. Pour in the stock and add the bay leaf, salt, and pepper. Bring to a boil. Reduce the heat to a simmer, add the peas, and cook until the peas are tender, about 10 minutes (5 minutes if using frozen peas). Remove the bay leaf and transfer the mixture to a blender. Add the tarragon, and purée. Return the soup to a clean saucepan if serving it warm, or pour it into a medium bowl, cover with plastic wrap, and refrigerate if serving it chilled.

caprese salad | In a large bowl, toss the red and yellow tomatoes and the mozzarella with the olive oil, salt, and pepper.

serve | Pour the soup into small glasses or sake cups, and place them on plates. Place 2 basil leaves on each plate, and arrange some of the salad on top of each leaf; garnish with small basil sprigs if you wish.

MAKE AHEAD The soup can be refrigerated up to 1 day before serving.

The tomatoes and cheese can be sliced, dressed, and refrigerated up to 2 hours ahead; let them stand at room temperature for 20 minutes before serving.

lobster under glass

SERVES 6

I love presenting classics in a new light, and this twist on Pheasant Under Glass (page 118) does just that, substituting one luxurious ingredient for another. Lobster, a timeless party standard, gets a fresh, modern edge from tomatillo salsa and tender corn cakes. You can boil the lobster yourself (8 to 8½ minutes for 1¼- to 1½-pound lobsters) or buy them pre-steamed at the supermarket. Serving the trio under a glass dome gives the dish a really elegant look (see opposite).

FOR THE CORN CAKES
⅓ cup yellow cornmeal
¼ cup all-purpose flour
1 cup roughly chopped fresh or thawed frozen corn
1 tablespoon finely chopped fresh chives
¾ teaspoon coarse salt
Freshly ground black pepper
2 large eggs
1 large egg yolk
¼ cup whole milk
4 tablespoons clarified butter (see Tip, page 83)

FOR SERVING
3 1¼- to 1½-pound lobsters, cooked, tail meat and claw meat removed
¼ cup extra-virgin olive oil
Grated zest of 1 lemon
½ teaspoon fine sea salt
½ cup tomatillo salsa, homemade (see page 74) or store-bought

corn cakes | In a large bowl, stir together the cornmeal, flour, chopped corn, chives, salt, and pepper. In a medium bowl, whisk together the eggs, egg yolk, milk, and 3 tablespoons of the clarified butter. Pour the liquid mixture over the dry ingredients and stir together with a spoon until they're well combined.

Heat an electric griddle to 325°F., or place a nonstick griddle or large nonstick skillet on the stovetop and heat it over medium heat. Grease the griddle with a little of the remaining 1 tablespoon clarified butter, and use about 1 tablespoon of the batter to make a silver-dollar-sized corn cake. Repeat with some more batter, cooking the corn cakes on both sides until golden, 1 to 2 minutes per side. Brush the griddle with more butter if needed, and cook the remaining batter. You should end up with 12 corn cakes. Use a spatula to transfer them to a plate.

serve | Place the lobster tail meat on a cutting board and chop it into 1-inch pieces. In a large bowl, whisk the olive oil, lemon zest, and salt together. Use a pastry brush to dab the seasoned oil onto the lobster meat. Divide the chopped lobster tail among six plates, mounding the meat slightly, and then lean a claw on top so the bottom of the claw is on the plate. Stack 3 corncakes on each plate and top with tomatillos salsa. Cover with a glass dome and serve.

MAKE AHEAD The salsa can be refrigerated for up to 1 day.

The cooked lobster can be shelled and refrigerated for up to 1 day.

The corn cakes can be made and refrigerated for 1 day or kept frozen for up to 1 week. Thaw at room temperature for a few hours and warm them for 2 minutes in a 350°F. oven before serving.

HORS D'OEUVRES
FOR BREAKFAST

Rice Krispy Canapés with Yogurt and Berries | Bagels and Lox

Scrambled Eggs and Bacon | Ham, Egg, and Cheese

Pancake Stacks | French Toast

Sugar Donuts | Oatmeal Crème Brûlée

AS A SPECIAL TREAT, MY MOM USED TO MAKE BREAKFAST for dinner for my sisters and me when we were kids. I absolutely loved it because the concept on its own was so unexpected—pancakes, French toast, or scrambled eggs for dinner? I like to keep this sense of surprise when I serve breakfast hors d'oeuvres—which, incidentally, aren't always served at breakfast time. Imagine how fun it is to close a party with coffee and donuts, or to pass mini bagels filled with lox and cream cheese alongside caviar cones and Champagne at a fancy party! Diminutive pancake stacks, scrambled egg and bacon canapés, and even French toast can be sleek and modern without sacrificing deliciousness for a picture-perfect presentation.

I can't help but think of Kate Spade whenever I try to brainstorm new breakfast hors d'oeuvres. For a decade we collaborated on breakfasts for her fashion company. During Fashion Week we'd host wonderfully imaginative breakfast receptions for her clients and the press to showcase her new collections. We'd dream up different foods and I'd coordinate the food to the theme. Kate would say, "Peter, your food *is* the entertainment!" Breakfast served in miniature always gives guests something new to talk about, whether in the wee hours of the morning or during the cocktail hour.

rice krispy canapés with yogurt and berries

MAKES 2 DOZEN

My ten-year-old daughter and I are both big cereal eaters, and she sometimes has hers with berries and yogurt instead of milk. Her morning routine inspired me to come up with this cereal bowl canapé filled with organic yogurt and topped with blueberries. It's fantastic as a breakfast hors d'oeuvre, but the sweetness of the cereal bowl (made with marshmallows) makes for an unexpected dessert, too.

Nonstick pan spray
1 tablespoon unsalted butter
6 large marshmallows
1 cup Rice Krispies cereal
½ cup vanilla organic yogurt
2 pints fresh blueberries

Lightly coat a 24-cup mini muffin tin with nonstick pan spray and set aside. In a small saucepan, melt the butter over low heat. Add the marshmallows and stir with a wooden spoon until they're completely melted. Turn off the heat and add the cereal, stirring until it's completely coated with marshmallow. Immediately spoon 1 teaspoon of the mixture into each cup of the prepared mini muffin tin, pressing the center gently to create a cup. (You need to work quickly so the mixture in the pan doesn't cool and harden.) Allow the mixture to set up for 1 minute before removing the bowls from the muffin tin.

Arrange the bowls on a platter, and fill each one with a little yogurt. Top with a few blueberries, and serve.

MAKE AHEAD The rice cereal bowls can be refrigerated in an airtight container for up to 2 days.

bagels and lox

MAKES 2 DOZEN

There are few foods that say "New York City" more than bagels and lox. We make our bagels in palm-sized portions for an unparalleled breakfast bite. A little dill mixed into the cream cheese gives them a fresh herby quality that perfectly complements the lox. Done in miniature, bagels become quite fancy and are a huge crowd-pleaser anytime, day or night.

FOR THE BAGELS
½ cup warm (about 110°F.) water
2 teaspoons sugar
1½ teaspoons malt syrup
2 teaspoons active dry yeast
1½ cups all-purpose flour, plus extra for shaping
½ teaspoon coarse salt
1 teaspoon vegetable oil
1 large egg
1 tablespoon sesame seeds

FOR SERVING
2 teaspoons finely chopped fresh dill (optional)
½ cup whipped cream cheese
1 pound thinly sliced lox, trimmed into 1½-inch-wide and 3-inch-long pieces

bagels | In a large bowl, whisk together the warm water, 1 teaspoon of the sugar, the malt syrup, and the yeast. Cover the bowl with plastic wrap and set it aside until the mixture becomes foamy, about 5 minutes.

Remove the plastic wrap and add 1¼ cups of the flour, a little at a time, mixing by hand until the ingredients come together. Add the salt and the remaining ¼ cup flour, if needed, mixing until the dough comes together as a stiff ball. Knead the dough in the bowl until it is smooth and not sticky, about 5 minutes.

Grease another large bowl with ½ teaspoon of the oil and place the dough ball in the bowl, turning it over to coat it with oil. Cover the bowl with plastic wrap and set it aside until the ball has doubled in size, about 1 hour.

Turn the dough out onto a lightly floured work surface and punch it down to deflate it. Roll the dough out into a ¼-inch-thick sheet, and then use a 1½-inch round cookie cutter to stamp out 24 rounds. Poke a finger through the center of each round to make a hole.

Grease a rimmed baking sheet with the remaining ½ teaspoon oil, and then place the shaped bagels on it. Cover loosely with a damp towel, and set aside until the bagels have doubled in size, 10 to 20 minutes (depending on how warm your kitchen is).

Meanwhile, preheat the oven to 375°F. Whisk the egg and 1 tablespoon water together in a small bowl, and set it aside.

Bring a large pot of water and the remaining 1 teaspoon sugar to a boil. Add about 6 bagels to the water and boil for about 45 seconds, using a slotted spoon or a frying spider to turn them while they boil. Return the bagels to the greased baking sheet and repeat with the remaining bagels.

(recipe continues)

Bake the bagels in the oven for 5 minutes. Remove the baking sheet from the oven, and use a spatula to flip the bagels. Brush the tops with the egg wash and sprinkle with the sesame seeds. Return the bagels to the oven and continue baking until they're golden brown, 10 to 15 minutes. Remove the baking sheet from the oven and let the bagels cool slightly; then transfer them to a wire rack to cool completely, about 30 minutes.

serve | Halve the bagels horizontally. Stir the dill (if using) into the cream cheese. Spread both cut sides of each bagel with a little cream cheese. Fold a piece of lox over and place it on top of the cream cheese. Place the seeded half on top, and serve.

MAKE AHEAD The bagels can be made 1 day ahead of serving. Store them in an airtight container at room temperature.

> TIP Instead of making your own mini bagels, buy pre-made ones at the supermarket, deli, or bagel shop (if they do minis).

homemade gravlax

MAKES 1 POUND

Gravlax is a traditional Scandinavian way of dry-curing salmon with dill and other herbs and spices. It's absolutely delicious and quite easy, and a nice way to really impress your guests. Tequila or limoncello lemon liqueur can be substituted for lemon juice if you prefer.

¼ cup roughly chopped fresh dill
¼ cup fresh cilantro leaves
½ cup packed light brown sugar
½ cup kosher salt
1 pound center-cut salmon (preferably in 1 piece), skin and pinbones removed
¼ cup fresh lemon juice (from about 1½ lemons)

Whisk the dill, cilantro, sugar, and salt together in a medium bowl. Place the salmon in a baking dish, sprinkle both sides with the lemon juice, and then pat both sides with the herb rub. Tightly wrap the salmon in plastic wrap and place it on a plate. Place another plate on top of the salmon and weigh it down with a can of tomatoes or beans. Refrigerate the salmon for at least 6 hours or up to 2 days. Before serving, unwrap the salmon, rinse off the spices, thinly slice crosswise, and serve.

scrambled eggs and bacon

MAKES 2 DOZEN

I love bacon and always have, perhaps because as kids we ate it only on weekends, which made it extra-special. Once we started spending our winter weekends and holidays skiing in Vermont, we began to discover all of the amazing thick-slab varieties sold in local markets and country stores. Great bacon is the key to a bacon-and-eggs hors d'oeuvre that transcends breakfast and is apropos at any time.

6 large eggs
3 tablespoons sour cream
1 tablespoon unsalted butter
Coarse salt and freshly ground black pepper
24 bacon cups (page 26)
2 tablespoons finely chopped fresh chives

In a medium bowl, lightly beat the eggs and 1 tablespoon of the sour cream until smooth. In a medium nonstick skillet, melt the butter over medium heat. Add the eggs, season with salt and pepper, reduce the heat to medium-low, and cook, stirring occasionally, until the eggs have set into large fluffy curds, 2 to 3 minutes. Taste for seasoning and add more salt or pepper if needed.

Divide the eggs among the bacon cups, sprinkle with the chives, and finish each with a dot of sour cream.

ham, egg, and cheese

MAKES 2 DOZEN

The ham, egg, and cheese sandwich is a classic New York City street vendor and bagel shop breakfast that tastes just as fabulous miniaturized and served at parties. We use Canadian bacon and trim English muffins down to a two-bite size and fill them with the same classic combo.

FOR THE ENGLISH MUFFINS AND HAM
8 English muffins, halved horizontally
12 ounces sliced Canadian bacon
12 ounces sliced cheddar cheese
2 tablespoons unsalted butter
1 teaspoon extra-virgin olive oil

FOR THE EGGS
6 large eggs
1 tablespoon sour cream
1 tablespoon unsalted butter
Coarse salt and freshly ground black pepper

english muffins and ham | Use a 1½-inch round cookie cutter to cut 24 rounds from the top halves of the English muffins, and 24 rounds from the bottom halves. Use the same cookie cutter to cut out 24 rounds of the Canadian bacon and 24 rounds of the cheese.

In a microwave-safe bowl, melt the butter. Use a pastry brush to brush the cut side of the English muffin tops and bottoms with the melted butter. Heat a large nonstick skillet over medium heat and place some of the muffin tops, buttered side down, in the skillet. Toast until browned, 1 to 2 minutes.

Repeat with the remaining muffins tops and bottoms. Set aside.

Heat another large nonstick skillet over medium heat. Add the olive oil and some of the Canadian bacon rounds, and brown the bacon on both sides, about 1 minute total. Transfer the bacon to a large plate and repeat with the remaining rounds. Set aside.

eggs | In a medium bowl, lightly beat the eggs and sour cream together until smooth. In a medium nonstick skillet, melt the butter over medium heat. Add the eggs, season with salt and pepper, reduce the heat to medium-low, and cook, stirring occasionally, until the eggs have set into large fluffy curds, 2 to 3 minutes. Taste for seasoning and add more salt or pepper if needed.

serve | Preheat the oven to 350°F.

Divide the scrambled eggs among the English muffin bottoms. Top each one with a cheese round and a bacon round. Cover with the English muffin tops and place on a rimmed baking sheet. Bake in the oven until warmed through, 1 to 2 minutes.

MAKE AHEAD The English muffin, cheese, and Canadian bacon rounds can be cut out 1 day ahead of serving. Store the muffins, covered with plastic wrap, at room temperature and the cheese and bacon in an airtight container in the refrigerator.

pancake stacks

MAKES 2 DOZEN

Kate Spade loves my silver-dollar-sized pancake stacks, laced with maple syrup and finished with a dollop of butter; they always end up on her Fashion Week party menus. I don't know anyone—fashionista or otherwise—who can resist their charm. Part of their appeal is that they're served in a tower, with the largest pancake on the bottom and a tiny dime-sized pancake on top. To simplify the cooking process, you can make the pancakes all the same size. If you like blueberry pancakes, add a few fresh berries to each pancake after you spoon the batter onto the griddle (if you stir the berries into the batter, the batter will turn blue!).

2 large eggs, separated
1 cup sour cream
4 tablespoons (½ stick) unsalted butter, melted,
    plus extra for cooking and serving
¼ teaspoon baking soda
2 cups all-purpose flour
1 tablespoon sugar
¼ teaspoon baking powder
¼ teaspoon coarse salt
2 tablespoons maple syrup

In a large bowl, whisk the egg yolks together until they're smooth. In a medium bowl, whisk together the sour cream, melted butter, and baking soda; then scrape this into the egg yolks and combine until smooth. In another medium bowl, whisk the flour, sugar, baking powder, and salt together. Use a rubber spatula to fold this into the sour cream mixture.

In a large bowl or the bowl of a stand mixer, whisk or beat the egg whites until stiff peaks form. Fold them into the batter until just a few white streaks remain.

Heat an electric griddle to 325°F., or place a nonstick griddle or large nonstick skillet on the stovetop and heat it over medium heat. Grease the griddle with a little butter and use about 1 tablespoon of the batter to make a quarter-sized pancake. Repeat so you have 24 quarter-sized pancakes (you'll probably have to cook them in a few batches), and cook on both sides until they're browned. Use a spatula to transfer them to a plate. Repeat, this time making 24 nickel-sized pancakes, and finally 24 dime-sized pancakes, buttering the griddle as needed.

Preheat the oven to 325°F. To make the stacks, place the largest pancakes on a rimmed baking sheet. Top each one with a pearl of maple syrup and cover it with a nickel-sized pancake. Top that with a dot of maple syrup, and add the last and smallest pancake. Repeat so you have 24 stacks.

Warm in the oven for up to 2 minutes, transfer the stacks to a platter, and serve with a pat of butter and more maple syrup on top.

MAKE AHEAD The stacks can be frozen on a baking sheet, then individually wrapped in plastic wrap and stored in a resealable freezer bag for up to 1 week.

TIP A squeeze bottle works well for squeezing out small amounts of maple syrup and for making the tiny dime-sized pancakes.

french toast

MAKES 2 DOZEN

We take the mini bread loaf that we make for grilled cheese sandwiches, slice it, dip the slices in French toast batter, and brown them. Sprinkled with confectioners' sugar, these are a classic breakfast offering. These were served at a *Breakfast at Tiffany's*–themed wedding for a segment Martha Stewart did on the *Today Show*.

4 large eggs
⅓ cup maple syrup
Grated zest and juice of 1 orange
1 teaspoon vanilla extract
¼ teaspoon ground cinnamon
½ teaspoon coarse salt
1 tablespoon unsalted butter, melted
1 mini loaf bread (page 53), cut into 24 ⅜-inch-thick slices
¼ cup confectioners' sugar

In a large bowl, whisk the eggs, maple syrup, and orange zest and juice together. Add the vanilla, cinnamon, and salt, and whisk to combine.

Preheat the oven to 325°F.

Heat a nonstick griddle to 325°F. and brush it with some melted butter, or brush a large nonstick skillet with melted butter and heat it over medium heat. One at a time, dip the bread slices in the batter, being sure to evenly coat both sides and letting the excess batter drip back into the bowl. Cook on the griddle until both sides are browned, 1 to 2 minutes per side. Transfer to a baking sheet and set aside.

Warm the French toast in the oven for 2 to 3 minutes, and then transfer it to a platter. Dust with the confectioners' sugar, and serve.

MAKE AHEAD The French toast can be refrigerated in an airtight container for up to 1 day. Reheat in a 350°F. oven for 2 to 3 minutes.

TIP Instead of making your own mini loaf of bread, use a 1½- or 2-inch cookie cutter to cut rectangles or squares from thin slices of store-bought white bread or brioche.

---

sugar donuts

MAKES 2 DOZEN

I've been going to Nantucket since my senior year in high school, when I spent a summer painting houses there. I'll never forget how every morning the entire community seemed to congregate at the Downyflake restaurant, from which the sugar-tinged smell of freshly fried dough wafted out and down the cobblestone streets. My sugar donut recipe is a direct descendant of my memories of the ones from the Downyflake.

4½ cups all-purpose flour, plus extra for rolling
4 teaspoons baking powder
½ teaspoon table salt
1 cup whole milk
1 cup sour cream
2 tablespoons unsalted butter, melted
1 teaspoon vanilla extract
1 teaspoon grated orange zest
2 large eggs
1 cup granulated sugar
6 cups vegetable oil
1 cup superfine sugar

In a large bowl, sift the flour, baking powder, and salt together. In a large liquid measuring cup, whisk together the milk, sour cream, melted butter, vanilla, and orange zest. Using a stand mixer or a hand mixer, beat the eggs and granulated sugar together on high speed until the mixture doubles in volume and is thick and pale yellow, about 3 minutes. Reduce the speed and slowly pour in the liquid ingredients, stopping the mixer to scrape the sides of the bowl as needed. With the mixer on low speed, add the dry ingredients in 3 additions, mixing until they are completely incorporated into the dough. The finished dough will be smooth and sticky. Use a rubber spatula to scrape the dough into a clean bowl. Cover it with plastic wrap and refrigerate the dough for 1 hour.

Turn the dough out onto a lightly floured work surface and roll it into a ⅜-inch-thick sheet. Use a 1½-inch round cookie cutter to stamp out as many rounds as you can from the dough. Use a ½-inch round cookie cutter to stamp a small round from the center of each larger one. Set the donut "holes" aside (see Tip, below).

In a large pot, heat the oil to 350°F. Add a few donuts (don't overcrowd the pot or the donuts will stick together and the oil will cool too quickly, yielding greasy donuts) and fry them until golden brown on both sides, about 1 minute total. Use a frying spider to transfer the donuts to a paper-towel-lined plate, and set aside. Repeat with the remaining donuts. Let the donuts cool until they're just warm to the touch.

Place the superfine sugar in a large bowl. Add a few warm donuts at a time and toss to coat in the sugar.

Arrange the donuts on a platter, or serve each one on the rim of a mug of freshly brewed coffee.

MAKE AHEAD The shaped donuts can be refrigerated on a baking sheet, covered with plastic wrap, for up to 1 day before frying.

TIP Fry the donut holes and eat them as a snack or for breakfast.

oatmeal crème brûlée

MAKES 2 DOZEN

My son loves crème brûlée and I love oatmeal, so one day it just popped into my head to combine these two dishes into one breakfast hors d'oeuvre. The sheath of brûléed sugar on top of the oatmeal raises its pedigree, making oatmeal sophisticated enough for even the toniest parties.

FOR THE OATMEAL
1 tablespoon unsalted butter
1 cup steel-cut oats
Pinch of coarse salt
1 cup whole milk or buttermilk
½ cup granola

FOR THE CRÈME BRÛLÉE
½ cup heavy cream
Grated zest of 1 orange
2 large egg yolks
½ teaspoon vanilla extract
½ cup plus 1½ tablespoons sugar

oatmeal | In a medium saucepan, bring 3 cups water to a boil. Melt the butter in a large pot. Stir in the oats and toast for 2 minutes, stirring often. Pour in the boiling water, add the salt, reduce the heat to a simmer, and cook, stirring often, until the oats begin to soften and thicken, about 20 minutes. Stir in the milk and continue to cook until the mixture is very rich and creamy and has the consistency of a thick pudding, 10 to 15 minutes. Spoon the oatmeal into twenty-four 1-ounce ramekins and sprinkle the granola on top. Cover with plastic wrap and refrigerate.

crème brûlée | Preheat the oven to 300°F.

In a medium saucepan, heat the cream and the orange zest over medium heat until it comes to a simmer. Reduce the heat to medium-low and simmer gently to infuse the orange zest flavor into the cream, about 15 minutes. Remove from the heat and strain into a medium bowl.

In another medium bowl, whisk the egg yolks and vanilla with the 1½ tablespoons sugar until the mixture is thick and pale yellow, about 2 minutes. Slowly whisk in the strained cream, and then divide the mixture between two 4-ounce ramekins.

Place the ramekins in an 8-inch baking dish or a small roasting pan, and set it on the oven rack. Pour hot water into the pan, taking care not to get any water in the ramekins, filling the pan until the water reaches halfway up the sides of the ramekins. Bake until the custard is just set around the edges and jiggles slightly in the middle, about 40 minutes. Carefully remove from the oven and set aside to cool in the water bath. Then remove the ramekins from the water bath, cover each one with plastic wrap, and refrigerate for at least 2 hours.

serve | Spread 2 tablespoons of the chilled custard over the granola in the ramekins. Evenly sprinkle 1 teaspoon of the remaining sugar over each serving, and place the ramekins on a rimmed baking sheet. Use a small blowtorch to caramelize the sugar, waving the torch over the sugar in a figure-8 pattern so it browns evenly. (Or preheat your broiler to high and place the rack 3 inches from the broiler element. Place the baking sheet under the broiler and broil until the sugar is caramelized, watching carefully to ensure the sugar doesn't burn.) Serve with a demitasse spoon.

MAKE AHEAD The oatmeal and the custard can be refrigerated for up to 2 days.

TIP Instead of making oatmeal from scratch, use instant oatmeal.

DESSERT

Fudgesicles | Sweet Frites | Chocolate Ice Cream "Burgers"

Milk and Cookies | Limoncello Popsicles | Chipwich Lollipops | Baked Alaskas

PB and Js | Cotton Candy Lollipops | Strawberry-Rhubarb Pies

Fluffernutters | Caramel Lady Apples with Chocolate Ganache Cores

Triple-Scoop Ice Cream Cones | S'Mores | Bagel Profiteroles | Pecan Tarts

FIST-SIZED TUFTS OF COTTON CANDY NESTED ON lollipop sticks. A milkshake shot with a fresh-baked soft chocolate chip cookie perched on the rim. This is how I do dessert: fun, fantastical, witty, and delicious. Before I created the concept of shrinking desserts into a bite and calling them hors d'oeuvres, catered desserts were typically served either on a dedicated dessert table or as a course to seated party-goers. At what other party will you see chocolate ice cream "burgers" and sweet frites (pages 175, 174) or one of my personal favorites, the Fluffernutter (page 194)? Now you can do this, too.

In addition to being cute, indulgent, and incredibly tasty, these bites boost the energy level at a party up a notch. Most often we pass them, meaning they're served savory-style throughout a room so guests don't have to stop dancing or end a conversation to go to the dessert table.

At home, you can pass them the way we do, or for smaller groups, present them on a stationary buffet or even on dessert plates for a seated course.

fudgesicles

MAKES 2 DOZEN

I like to serve chocolatey Fudgesicles alongside the Limoncello Popsicles (page 181) for a striking presentation—they are the perfect nonalcoholic retro partner.

1 2-ounce package chocolate instant pudding mix, such as Jell-O
½ cup sugar
½ cup heavy cream
2 cups whole milk
24 3 x ⅜-inch popsicle sticks

In a medium bowl, whisk the instant pudding mix, sugar, cream, and milk together. Pour the mixture into a mini popsicle mold or two ice cube trays (fill the cubes three-quarters full). Freeze until the liquid is partially frozen, about 2 hours, and then insert the popsicle sticks. Freeze until fully frozen, about 1 hour longer.

Carefully remove the popsicles from the molds and place them on a platter, or stand them up in a block of Styrofoam, and serve.

MAKE AHEAD The popsicles can be frozen up to 2 weeks ahead.

sweet frites

MAKES 2 DOZEN

I like to serve these with the Chocolate Ice Cream "Burgers," opposite. They're also great on their own. To dress up the presentation, serve them in person-alized cones; see page 235 for ideas. *(Pictured on page 176.)*

½ cup plus 2 tablespoons sugar
2½ tablespoons ground cinnamon
1 teaspoon vanilla extract
1 teaspoon grated lemon zest
¼ teaspoon table salt
8 tablespoons (1 stick) unsalted butter
1 cup all-purpose flour
3 large eggs
6 cups vegetable oil

In a medium bowl, whisk the ½ cup sugar and the cinnamon together. Set aside.

In a medium pot, stir together 1 cup water, the remaining 2 tablespoons sugar, and the vanilla, lemon zest, and salt. Add the butter and bring to a boil, stirring occasionally. Using a heatproof rubber spatula or a wooden spoon, stir in the flour (don't reduce the heat), stirring until it forms a ball, about 3 minutes. Transfer the dough to the bowl of a stand mixer (or a large bowl if using a hand mixer).

Beating the dough on medium speed, add the eggs, one at a time, waiting until each is completely incorporated before adding the next. Scrape the batter into a pastry bag fitted with a small round tip.

In a large pot, heat the oil to 350°F. Pipe some of the batter into the oil in 4-inch-long strips (use a knife or scissors to cut the batter off the tip as it comes out). Cook the churros in batches, using a frying spider or tongs to turn them over occasionally, until all sides are golden brown, about 1 minute. Transfer to a paper-towel-lined baking sheet and immediately sprinkle with the cinnamon-sugar.

Serve hot or at room temperature, in paper cones (see page 42).

MAKE AHEAD The batter can be made 1 day ahead and refrigerated, covered. Let it sit out at room temperature for 2 hours before filling the pastry bag.

chocolate ice cream "burgers"

MAKES 2 DOZEN

I thought it would be fun to come up with a dessert version of the mini burger that's the spitting image of its savory cousin. Meringue "buns" are the perfect bookends for a chocolate ice cream "patty," and to further push the image, I serve them alongside Sweet Frites, a cone of slender churro "fries," opposite. It's such a convincing presentation that many guests actually do a double take!

FOR THE MERINGUE BUNS
¾ cup sliced almonds
2 tablespoons confectioners' sugar
2 large egg whites
¼ teaspoon cream of tartar
Pinch of table salt
¼ teaspoon vanilla extract
1 tablespoon poppy seeds
¼ cup bittersweet chocolate chips

FOR THE BURGERS
1 pint good-quality chocolate ice cream
6 large fresh strawberries, hulled and sliced crosswise ⅜-inch thick
24 fresh mint leaves

buns | In a food processor, grind the almonds with 1 tablespoon of the confectioners' sugar until the mixture is fine. Add the remaining 1 tablespoon confectioners' sugar and process until powdery. Set aside.

Using a stand mixer or hand mixer set to medium speed, whip the egg whites until they are foamy, about 1 minute. With the mixer running, add the cream of tartar and the salt, and beat until the whites hold stiff peaks, 1 to 2 minutes. Turn off the mixer and use a rubber spatula to fold the ground almonds into the egg whites. Once the almonds are almost completely incorporated, add the vanilla and fold it in until the mixture is combined.

Line two baking sheets with parchment paper. Use a pencil and a 1½-inch round cookie cutter to trace 24 circles, 1½ inches apart, onto each sheet of paper. Flip the parchment paper pencil-side down on the baking sheets. Spoon 1 heaping teaspoon of the egg white mixture into the center of each circle. Sprinkle the poppy seeds on top of the whites on one baking sheet (these will be the burger tops). Leave both baking sheets out at room temperature for 4 hours.

Preheat the oven to 300°F.

Bake the meringues for 5 minutes. Raise the temperature to 450°F., and bake for an additional 7 minutes. Remove from the oven and let cool. Once cool, peel the meringues off the paper and place them on a wire rack.

In a small microwave-safe bowl, microwave the chocolate chips in 15-second increments, stirring after each, until they're completely melted. Use a pastry brush or butter knife to spread some chocolate on the flat side of each meringue (this prevents the ice cream from softening the meringue).

(recipe continues)

burgers | Let the ice cream sit out at room temperature for 10 to 20 minutes, or until the sides of the container are soft when squeezed. Place the pint on top of a parchment-paper-lined baking sheet. Use a rubber spatula to remove the ice cream from the container, and turn it out onto the paper. Cover with another sheet of parchment and use your hands to press it into a flat $3/8$-inch-thick sheet. Place the baking sheet in the freezer and chill until the ice cream is frozen solid, at least 2 hours. Once frozen, use a $1\frac{1}{2}$-inch round cookie cutter to stamp out the burgers.

serve | Place the bottom buns (without poppy seeds), chocolate side up, on your work surface and layer each with a strawberry slice, then a mint leaf, and set the chocolate "burger" on top of the mint. Cover with the poppy-seed top bun. Serve immediately.

MAKE AHEAD The chocolate-coated meringue buns can be made up to 2 days ahead and stored in an airtight container in a cool, dry place.

The ice cream burgers can be cut out and kept frozen in an airtight container or gallon-sized resealable freezer bag for up to 2 weeks.

TIPS Use store-bought meringue cookies for the buns instead of making your own.

To dress up your mini ice cream burger offer chocolate sauce on the side in a bowl with a small paintbrush.

Consider butterscotch and strawberry sauce, too.

Make your burger out of coffee ice cream or toffee ice cream.

milk and cookies

MAKES 2 DOZEN

I attended a few different colleges in the process of finding my calling. While I was at the University of Vermont, I frequented its amazing dairy bar, where they made the best milkshakes, and where my love of milkshakes began. What makes my version extra-special (besides its two-sip size) is the chewy and totally decadent cookie perched on the rim of the glass. The key is to underbake the cookies so they retain that just-baked softness.

FOR THE COOKIES
1 cup plus 2 tablespoons all-purpose flour
½ teaspoon baking soda
½ teaspoon salt
2 tablespoons unsalted butter, at room temperature
½ cup granulated sugar
½ cup (packed) light brown sugar
1 large egg
½ teaspoon vanilla extract
1½ cups mini chocolate chips

FOR THE MILKSHAKE
1 quart (4 cups) whole milk
1 cup vanilla ice cream
1 teaspoon vanilla extract

cookies | In a medium bowl, whisk the flour, baking soda, and salt together. Set aside.

In the bowl of a stand mixer (or a large bowl if using a hand mixer), cream the butter, granulated sugar, and light brown sugar together until creamy and smooth. Add the egg and vanilla, and beat until incorporated. Add the flour mixture, combine on low speed for 1 minute, and then add the chocolate chips, stirring until they're mixed in. Cover the bowl with plastic wrap and refrigerate for at least 1 hour.

Preheat the oven to 350°F.

Line a rimmed baking sheet with parchment-paper, and scoop ½-teaspoon balls of dough, placing them 2 inches apart on the baking sheet. Bake until the edges of the cookies are set, about 7 minutes. Remove from the oven, let cool for 1 minute, and then use a spatula to transfer them to a cutting board. While the cookies are still warm, use a paring knife to make a ½-inch slit into the side of each cookie so it can sit on the rim of the shake.

milkshake | Put the milk, ice cream, and vanilla in a blender jar and blend until smooth.

serve | Divide the milkshake among twenty-four small shot glasses. Balance a cookie on each rim, and serve with a straw (the straws might need to be trimmed with scissors so they're not too long).

MAKE AHEAD The cookie dough can be prepared, wrapped in plastic, and refrigerated for up to 2 days.

The cookies can be baked up to 3 days before serving. Store them in an airtight container at room temperature.

> **TIP** Instead of making your own, use store-bought cookie dough to make the cookies.

limoncello popsicles

MAKES 2 DOZEN

I had the idea to shrink the popsicle long before we actually figured out how to do it. The concept sounds easy, but it was actually quite hard to find someone to make the mold for us in quantities less than 100,000! It took a *Martha Stewart Weddings* deadline to finally make the mini pops a reality. We found a sculptor and made a prototype from clay before the real deal was created (at home, you can use a mini popsicle mold or an ice cube tray). I make these with limoncello, an Italian Day-Glo-yellow lemon-flavored liqueur, for an adult version of the kid classic.

¼ cup sugar
1 cup fresh lemon juice (from about 4 lemons)
⅓ cup fresh orange juice (from about 1 orange)
½ cup limoncello liqueur
24 3 x ⅜-inch popsicle sticks

In a small saucepan, bring ¼ cup water and the sugar to a boil, stirring occasionally to dissolve the sugar. Turn off the heat and set aside to cool.

Pour the cooled simple syrup, lemon juice, orange juice, and limoncello into a pitcher and stir to combine. Pour the mixture into a mini popsicle mold or two ice cube trays (fill the cubes three-quarters full). Freeze until the liquid is partially frozen, about 2 hours, and then insert the popsicle sticks. Freeze until fully frozen, about 1 hour longer.

Carefully remove the popsicles from the molds and place them on a platter, or stand them up in a block of Styrofoam, and serve.

MAKE AHEAD The popsicles can be frozen up to 2 weeks ahead.

DIY Popsicle Serving Tray | Make your own popsicle serving tray using a 2-inch-thick rectangular block of Styrofoam. Wrap the block with decorative paper (make sure the seam is on the bottom). Then, using a sharp paring knife, make ½-inch-long and 1-inch-deep slits in the block. Wedge the popsicle sticks into the slits to serve upright.

chipwich lollipops

MAKES 2 DOZEN

Though chocolate chip cookies and vanilla ice cream are somewhat commonplace, once you miniaturize the cookies, sandwich them with good-quality ice cream, and then stick them on a lollipop stick, you have created a whole new riff on the ice cream sandwich.

48 chocolate chip cookies (see page 178; double the recipe and skip the notch step)
½ cup good-quality vanilla ice cream, slightly softened
24 lollipop sticks

Place 24 cookies, flat side up, on your work surface. Place 1 teaspoon of the ice cream on each cookie and cover with the remaining cookies, flat side down. Press the cookies together gently with enough pressure so the ice cream spreads out to sandwich them together but doesn't squish out. Push a lollipop stick halfway into the ice cream, and freeze for at least 30 minutes.

Place the lollipops on a platter, or stand them up in a block of Styrofoam, and serve.

MAKE AHEAD The Chipwiches can be made and frozen up to 2 weeks before serving.

TIP Instead of making the chocolate chip cookies from scratch, use packaged cookies (preferably the smallest ones you can find) to make the lollipops.

More Cookie-Based Ice Cream Lollipops | Why stop
with Chipwiches when there are so many ways to serve mini ice cream sandwiches? Here are some more cookie options for ice cream lollipops.

- Oreo cookies (separate the cookies and remove the filling first)
- Gingersnaps
- Nilla wafers
- Pecan sandies

baked alaskas

MAKES 2 DOZEN

When you add sparklers to a dessert, it instantly becomes so much more celebratory. We use them just as you would birthday candles and for all sorts of occasions—birthdays, weddings, anniversaries, bar and bat mitzvahs, and even just to dress up a simple, classic ice cream dessert like this meringue-covered Baked Alaska. For bite-sized desserts, we use 5-inch-tall sparklers with a 3-inch wick.

FOR THE CAKE

3 tablespoons unsalted butter: 1 tablespoon at room temperature, 2 tablespoons melted
3 large eggs
½ cup plus 1 teaspoon sugar
½ teaspoon vanilla extract
½ cup cake flour, plus extra for cake pan

FOR THE MERINGUE

2 large egg whites
½ cup sugar
¼ teaspoon cream of tartar

FOR THE BAKED ALASKAS

¼ cup dark rum
24 ½-ounce (1-tablespoon) scoops vanilla ice cream

cake | Preheat the oven to 350°F. Grease a 9 × 12-inch baking dish with the room-temperature butter. Add about 2 tablespoons flour and shake the dish to evenly coat it, and then tap out and discard the excess flour.

Place the eggs in a large heatproof bowl. Fill a medium saucepan with 1 inch of water and bring it to a simmer over medium-high heat. Reduce the heat to medium-low, and place the bowl over the simmering water (make sure the bottom of the bowl doesn't touch the water). Whisk the eggs until they're lukewarm, about 2 minutes. Then whisk in ⅓ cup of the sugar and beat until the sugar is dissolved. Remove the bowl from the saucepan, turn off the heat, and transfer the mixture to the bowl of a stand mixer (or keep it in the large bowl if using a hand mixer). Beat on medium speed until the eggs are very thick and pale, about 7 minutes. Add the remaining sugar and continue to beat until the eggs are a pale lemon color, 1 to 2 minutes. Add the vanilla and beat for 1 minute. Using a rubber spatula, fold in the cake flour. When just a few streaks remain, pour in the melted butter and gently fold it in.

Pour the batter into the prepared baking dish and bake until a toothpick inserted into the center comes out clean, 25 to 30 minutes. Remove from the oven and set aside to cool. Reduce the oven temperature to 250°F.

meringue | Place a 10 × 15-inch piece of parchment paper (or a piece of parchment the size of your baking sheet) on your work surface. Use a 1½-inch round cookie cutter and a pencil to trace 24 circles on the parchment, spacing them about 1 inch apart. Flip the parchment paper pencil-side down on a baking sheet, and set it aside.

In the bowl of a stand mixer (or in a medium bowl if using a hand mixer), beat 1 egg white until it is foamy. Then, while beating, slowly sprinkle in ¼ cup of the sugar followed by ⅛ teaspoon of the cream of tartar. Continue to beat until the mixture forms stiff peaks (when the beater is pulled out, the meringue stands in a straight peak). Scrape the meringue into a pastry bag fitted with a small round tip, or into a squeeze bottle, and pipe the meringue onto the parchment paper, forming 24 flat disks the size of the circles.

Bake the meringues until they are dry and firm, 1 to 1½ hours (they should remain white). Remove from the oven and set aside. (When they are fully cooled, store in an airtight container.)

(recipe continues)

Beat the remaining egg white in a clean bowl until frothy. Gradually add the remaining ¼ cup sugar, followed by the remaining ⅛ teaspoon cream of tartar, and continue beating until stiff peaks form. Scrape the mixture into a pastry bag fitted with a small round tip.

baked alaskas | Use a 1½-inch round cookie cutter to cut the cake into 24 rounds. Pour the rum into a small dish, and use a pastry brush to dab a little rum onto each cake round. Place a scoop of ice cream on top of each cake round, and pipe the meringue around the ice cream and the cake base. Cover with plastic wrap and freeze overnight.

serve | Just before serving, pull the baked Alaskas from the freezer. Set each meringue-covered ice cream and cake on top of a meringue base, and place it on a dessert plate. Use a kitchen blowtorch to brown the meringue. Insert a sparkler into each baked Alaska, light, and serve.

MAKE AHEAD The meringue bases can be stored in an airtight container at room temperature for up to 1 week.

The cake can be baked and the rounds cut out up to 2 days ahead. Store in an airtight container.

The baked Alaskas can be assembled and kept frozen for up to 1 day. Wait to brown the meringue just before serving.

TIPS Instead of making meringue bases, use store-bought meringue cookies for the base.

Instead of making cake from scratch, slice a store-bought pound cake lengthwise into ¼-inch-thick pieces and cut out the cake rounds from the slices.

pb and js

MAKES 4 DOZEN

After turning the burger into a dessert (see page 175), I came up with the next savory-becomes-sweet treat. I'm a big fan of peanut-butter-and-jelly sandwiches, so I started playing with the concept and devised a new version: pound cake, sweetened peanut butter cream, melted bittersweet chocolate, and raspberry jam. The finished sandwich looks just like the brown-bag classic, which is half the fun! See page 250 for sources of mini loaf pans.

FOR THE POUND CAKE
1 cup (2 sticks) plus 2 tablespoons unsalted butter, at room temperature
2 cups plus 2 tablespoons all-purpose flour
Grated zest of 1 orange
¼ teaspoon cream of tartar
¼ teaspoon fine salt
1 cup sugar
5 large eggs, at room temperature
½ teaspoon vanilla extract

FOR THE JELLY
¾ cup raspberry or strawberry jam
1 tablespoon cornstarch

FOR THE PEANUT BUTTER CREAM
1 cup smooth peanut butter
5 tablespoons unsalted butter, at room temperature
1 cup confectioners' sugar
⅓ cup heavy cream
¼ teaspoon coarse salt
⅓ cup milk
3 tablespoons cornstarch

FOR THE CHOCOLATE
8 ounces bittersweet chocolate, finely chopped

pound cake | Preheat the oven to 325°F. Grease two 2¼ × 11¾-inch loaf pans with the 2 table-spoons butter. Add 1 tablespoon of the flour to each pan, and shake and tap to evenly coat the bottom and sides. Shake out the excess flour and set the pans aside.

In the bowl of a stand mixer (or a large bowl if using a hand mixer), cream the remaining 1 cup butter on medium-high speed until it has doubled in volume and is very pale, about 10 minutes.

Meanwhile, sift the remaining 2 cups flour into a medium bowl, and stir in the orange zest, cream of tartar, and salt.

Reduce the mixer speed to low, and slowly sprinkle in the sugar. Beat for 5 minutes. Then add the eggs, one at a time, beating after each addition to ensure it is completely incorporated before adding the next (use a rubber spatula to scrape the bottom and sides of the bowl as necessary). Then add the vanilla and mix to combine. Turn off the mixer, and using a rubber spatula, gently fold in the dry ingredients. Take care not to overmix the batter.

Use a rubber spatula to scrape the batter into the prepared loaf pans. Bake until a cake tester inserted into the center comes out clean, about 1 hour. Remove the cakes from the oven and set them aside to cool completely, about 2 hours. Once cool, invert the pans, remove the cakes, and flip them over right-side up on a cutting board. Cut off the ends from each loaf and slice the cakes into ¼-inch-thick pieces. Cut the slices into 2-inch squares (you need 48 total). Set aside.

jelly | In a small saucepan, heat the jam over medium heat until it is liquefied and mostly smooth. Continue to simmer gently until the jam thickens, about 5 minutes.

In a small bowl, stir together the cornstarch and 1 tablespoon water until the cornstarch is completely dissolved. Stir the cornstarch slurry into the hot jam, and whisk constantly until the jam becomes very thick, 4 to 5 minutes. Line a 12 × 17-inch rimmed baking sheet with parchment

(recipe continues)

paper, and scrape the jam onto it. Cover with plastic wrap and refrigerate until the jam is cold and solid, about 2 hours. Remove the jam from the refrigerator and cut it into twenty-four 2-inch squares.

peanut butter cream | Place the peanut butter, butter, confectioners' sugar, cream, and salt in a large bowl (or the bowl of a stand mixer) and beat until smooth. In a small bowl, whisk the milk and cornstarch together until the cornstarch is completely dissolved. Add the cornstarch slurry to the peanut butter mixture, and beat on medium speed until well combined, about 1 minute.

Use a rubber spatula to transfer the peanut butter cream to a 12 × 17-inch rimmed baking sheet, smoothing the top to make the layer as even as possible. Refrigerate until just firm enough to cut into squares, about 30 minutes. Use a paring knife to cut out twenty-four 2-inch squares, and then return the pan to the refrigerator.

chocolate | Place the chocolate in a microwave-safe bowl and microwave it in 20-second increments, stirring after each, until it is completely melted, about 2 minutes. Line a 12 × 17-inch rimmed baking sheet with parchment paper and scrape the chocolate onto the parchment, using an offset spatula to spread it into an even layer. Cover with plastic wrap and refrigerate it until it is cool enough to cleanly slice but not hard and brittle, about 15 minutes. Slice the chocolate into twenty-four 2-inch squares.

serve | Place 24 cake squares on a cutting board. Top each with a chocolate square, a peanut butter square, a jam square, and finally another cake square. Slice the squares in half on the diagonal so you have 48 triangles. Place on a rimmed baking sheet, cover with plastic wrap, and refrigerate until serving.

To serve, arrange the PB and Js on a tray so you can see all the layers and let them sit out for 10 minutes before serving.

MAKE AHEAD All of the components—cake, peanut butter cream, jelly, and chocolate—can be refrigerated for up to 3 days before serving (wrap the cake tightly in two layers of plastic wrap so it doesn't dry out).

The PB and Js can be assembled and refrigerated several hours before serving.

TIP Use store-bought pound cake instead of making your own.

cotton candy lollipops

MAKES 2 DOZEN

After reading that cotton candy was served to a customer on a small dessert plate as a gift from the chef at a New York City restaurant, I envisioned pink cotton candy clouds floating atop lollipop sticks at the choicest gatherings. I served these Cotton Candy Lollipops at a party thrown by Dylan Lauren (of Dylan's Candy Bar—and Ralph Lauren's daughter). Then her brother David asked me to make them for his party, and before I knew it, they had become a staple at my fanciest weddings and fashion fêtes. Cotton candy machines can be rented through a party rental supply company.

1 cup sugar
3 to 4 drops red food coloring (depends on the brand of food coloring used)
24 lollipop sticks

Follow the instructions on the cotton candy machine to make the cotton candy. (Plan on about 2 minutes per serving.)

Gather plum-sized tufts of cotton candy and place each on top of a lollipop stick. Serve immediately.

MAKE AHEAD Cotton candy can be made 1 day ahead and stored in a plastic bag at room temperature.

> **TIP** Don't make cotton candy on a humid day—it will melt immediately!

strawberry-rhubarb pies

MAKES 2 DOZEN

Pies are all about summer and roadside farm stands brimming with baskets of ruby-red field-grown berries. I spent many summers at my grandparents' farmhouse in the Hamptons, and strawberry-rhubarb pie brings me right back. We make our mini version with either a crisscross lattice top crust or a quick and delicious crumb topping.

FOR THE PIE SHELLS
1½ cups all-purpose flour, plus extra for rolling
1½ tablespoons sugar
½ teaspoon salt
2½ tablespoons solid vegetable shortening
1 tablespoon unsalted butter, cut into small bits
3 tablespoons ice water
1½ cups dried beans, for pie weights

FOR THE PIES
6 cups diced fresh rhubarb
6 tablespoons fresh orange juice (from about 1 orange)
2 tablespoons grated lemon zest (from 2 large lemons)
1½ tablespoons sugar
1 tablespoon ground cinnamon
1 tablespoon ground cloves
3 cups diced fresh strawberries
1 tablespoon cornstarch
1 large egg, lightly beaten
Sweetened whipped cream, for serving (optional)

pie shells | In a food processor, pulse the flour, sugar, and salt together to combine. Add the shortening and butter, and pulse until crumbly with no bits larger than a small pea. With the machine running, add the ice water, 1 tablespoon at a time, until the dough forms a ball (don't let the dough mix for more than 1 minute once you start adding water). Turn the dough out onto your work surface and divide it in half. Flatten each half into a disk and wrap them in plastic wrap. Refrigerate overnight.

Lightly flour your work surface. Roll 1 dough disk into a ⅜-inch-thick sheet (it doesn't have to be round). Use a 3-inch round cookie cutter to cut out 24 rounds. Press each round into a 2-inch tart pan with removable bottom, pinching off any overhang. Repeat with the other dough disk. Press the dough scraps together into a disk, wrap in plastic wrap, and refrigerate.

Prick the bottom of each crust a few times with a fork. Place the tart pans on a rimmed baking sheet and refrigerate for 15 minutes.

Meanwhile, preheat the oven to 350°F. Cut out twenty-four 3-inch squares of aluminum foil.

Remove the baking sheet from the refrigerator and fit each pie shell with a square of foil. Add about 1 tablespoon dried beans to each shell (to prevent the dough from shrinking). Bake until the edges are golden brown, 22 to 24 minutes.

While the crusts are baking, make the lattice tops: On a lightly floured work surface, roll the reserved scraps into a ⅜-inch-thick sheet. Use a pizza cutter or a knife to cut the dough into ¼-inch-wide, 2-inch-long strips (you'll need 144 strips total). Transfer them to a parchment-paper-lined baking sheet and refrigerate until needed.

Remove the pie crusts from the oven and let them cool completely before removing the foil and beans. (Place the beans in a jar and reuse them the next time you have to prebake pie shells.)

pies | Make the filling: In a large skillet, combine the rhubarb, orange juice, lemon zest, sugar, cinnamon, and cloves. Bring to a boil over medium-high heat, stirring occasionally. In a medium bowl, toss the strawberries with the cornstarch; add them to the skillet. Reduce the heat to medium and continue cooking until

(recipe continues)

the mixture is as thick as jam, about 4 minutes. Transfer to a medium bowl and set aside to cool completely.

Preheat the oven to 350°F.

Fill each pie crust with 1 tablespoon of the strawberry-rhubarb filling. Remove the dough strips from the refrigerator. Dip 3 strips into the beaten egg and arrange them ⅜-inch apart across the top of a pie, pressing the ends onto the tart pan to seal. Dip another 3 strips in the beaten egg and place them on top of the pie, going in the opposite direction of the first 3 strips. Press off the ends and place the pie on a rimmed baking sheet. Repeat with the remaining dough strips and pie crusts. Bake the pies until golden, about 14 minutes. Remove from the oven and set aside to cool.

serve | Remove the pies from the tart pans, and serve with a dollop of whipped cream if desired.

MAKE AHEAD The pie dough can be refrigerated, wrapped in plastic wrap, for up to 4 days or frozen for up to 1 month. The pie shells can be baked up to 2 days in advance.

The filling can be refrigerated for up to 2 days.

The pies can be baked 1 day before serving. Store them at room temperature.

TIP Use store-bought pie dough instead of making your own.

VARIATION
crumb topping

In a food processor, pulse together ⅓ cup all-purpose flour, ½ cup (packed) light brown sugar, and 4 tablespoons cold unsalted butter (cut into small cubes) until the mixture is crumbly. Instead of making the lattice top, sprinkle a little over each pie and bake as instructed.

woven-lattice crust

For a woven-lattice top crust, place one pie dough strip diagonally across the center of the pie, with the top of the strip at the upper-left corner and the bottom of the strip at the lower-right corner. Place a second strip of dough in the opposite direction from the first, diagonally over the top third of the pie, with the bottom part of the strip at the mid-left edge and the top part of the strip on the upper-right edge. Place a third strip of dough over the second strip, with the top of the third strip at the top center of the pie, crossing diagonally to the mid-right edge of the pie. Place the top of the fourth strip over the third strip at the upper-left corner of the pie with the lower end of the strip at the lower-left side of the pie. The fifth and last strip of dough runs diagonally over the lower-left side of the pie. Pinch off the dough overhang and proceed with the remaining strips and pies.

fluffernutters

MAKES 2 DOZEN

The Fluffernutter is one of my first (and best) food memories. When I was four years old, I'd go to my friend and next-door neighbor's house to play. Her mom made us Fluffernutter sandwiches from Marshmallow Fluff and peanut butter—to this day, a perfect snack. People can't believe it when we bring these out at highbrow events. In their toasted cones, they're a very original adaptation.

FOR THE CONES
12 thin slices white sandwich bread, crusts removed

FOR THE FLUFFERNUTTERS
2 cups confectioners' sugar
24 marshmallows
½ cup creamy peanut butter

cones | Preheat the oven to 350°F.

Place a bread slice on your work surface and use a rolling pin to flatten it to ⅜-inch thickness. Slice the piece in half diagonally, and wrap a half around a #800 pastry tip. Then insert it inside another pastry tip to hold the bread in place. Repeat with the remaining pastry tips (if you have twelve tips, you will be able to make 6 cones at a time). Place the cones on a rimmed baking sheet and bake until golden, about 5 minutes. Cool for 5 minutes before removing the bread cones from the tips. Repeat with the remaining bread slices.

fluffernutters | Place the confectioners' sugar in small bowl. Roll a marshmallow in the sugar to evenly coat it, rolling and pressing it into a 1-inch ball. Place the marshmallow on an aluminum-foil-lined baking sheet. Repeat with the remaining marshmallows.

Set an oven rack at the top position (about 3 inches from the broiler element) and heat the broiler to high. Place the baking sheet in the oven and broil until the marshmallows are lightly browned, 15 to 30 seconds (watch your broiler closely, as heat intensity varies). Or, if you have a kitchen blowtorch, torch the marshmallows until browned.

serve | Fill each cone with 1 teaspoon of the peanut butter, and place 1 browned marshmallow on top. Serve immediately.

MAKE AHEAD The bread cones can be toasted up to 3 days in advance. Store them in an airtight container in a cool, dry place.

caramel lady apples with chocolate ganache cores

Caramel apples look great but often are too much of a good thing, which is why making them out of petite Lady apples is a perfect party solution. Most of the time I like people to know exactly what to expect by the appearance of an hors d'oeuvre, but in this case, guests get a bit of a surprise when they bite into the apple to discover a chocolate ganache filling instead of an apple core.

FOR THE GANACHE
8 ounces bittersweet or semisweet chocolate, finely chopped
¾ cup heavy cream
2 tablespoons unsalted butter, at room temperature

FOR THE LADY APPLES
24 Lady apples (or other very small red apples)
24 medium-thick 6-inch twigs (or lollipop sticks)
1 14-ounce box caramel apple kit (see Resources, page 250)
Hot Mulled Cider (page 231), for serving

ganache | Place the chocolate in a medium bowl and set aside. Bring the cream to a simmer in a small saucepan over high heat and then pour it over the chocolate. Cover the bowl with plastic wrap and set aside for 5 minutes. Uncover the bowl and whisk the cream and chocolate together until semi-smooth, add the butter, and continue to gently whisk until the mixture comes together and is completely smooth.

lady apples | Place the apples upside-down on your work surface. Use an apple corer to remove half of each core, and then scoop out any remaining seeds with a small melon baller. Fill each center with about 1 tablespoon of the ganache. Place the apples on a parchment-paper-lined rimmed baking sheet and refrigerate for 1 hour.

Remove the apples from the refrigerator and turn them stem side up. Insert a twig into each apple top (where the stem is—or was). Melt the caramel according to the package instructions. Hold an apple by the twig and dip it halfway into the caramel (make sure the caramel isn't too warm; otherwise it could melt the chocolate core). Place the apple back onto the baking sheet, upside-down with the twig sticking up. Repeat with the remaining apples.

Refrigerate the apples until serving, with mulled cider on the side.

MAKE AHEAD The apples can be made and refrigerated up to 1 day before serving.

TIP If it's humid or rainy, don't try making these—the caramel won't set up properly.

---

triple-scoop ice cream cones

MAKES 2 DOZEN

Most often it's an image of food that inspires a new hors d'oeuvre. In this case, it's those cartoons of impossibly tall ice cream cones with half a dozen scoops teetering on top of a teeny-tiny cone. This is my rendition, with three manageable scoops of classic ice cream flavors like mint chocolate chip, chocolate, and strawberry. See page 250 for a source of a mini waffle cone maker.

FOR THE CONES
2 cups all-purpose flour
1 teaspoon sugar
½ teaspoon baking powder
½ teaspoon table salt
¼ cup nonfat dry milk
⅓ cup solid vegetable shortening
¼ cup light corn syrup
1 large egg
2 tablespoons vegetable oil

FOR THE ICE CREAM
1½ cups good-quality mint chocolate chip ice cream
1½ cups good-quality chocolate ice cream
1½ cups good-quality strawberry ice cream

cones | In a large bowl, sift together the flour, sugar, baking powder, and salt. Stir in the dry milk, and then add the shortening. Using a pastry cutter or your hands, blend the shortening into the dry ingredients until the mixture is sandy in texture. Whisk in 1 cup water, stirring the mixture until it is smooth.

In a medium bowl, whisk together the corn syrup, egg, and oil. Add this to the batter, beating until it is smooth. Set the batter aside to rest for 10 minutes.

Prepare a mini waffle cone maker according to the manufacturer's instructions. Spoon 1 teaspoon of the batter into each mold of the waffle iron, and cook until browned. Remove the waffles from the machine and fold into a cone shape, following the manufacturer's instructions. Repeat with the rest of the batter.

ice cream | Use a ½-ounce scoop or a tablespoon to portion out 24 balls of each flavor of ice cream. Place the scoops on a parchment-lined baking sheet (if using a small baking sheet, you'll need two) and freeze for at least 1 hour.

serve | Remove the ice cream from the freezer and let it sit out for 5 to 10 minutes to soften slightly. Then stack 3 balls together (1 ball of each flavor), set each triple-scoop stack of ice cream on top of a cone, and serve immediately.

MAKE AHEAD The cones can be stored in an airtight container at room temperature for up to 3 days.

The ice cream can be scooped, placed on a parchment-paper-lined baking sheet, covered with plastic wrap, and frozen up to 4 days in advance of serving.

s'mores

MAKES 2 DOZEN

Everyone has their own special s'mores memory. Mine is of summertime in Wainscott, Long Island, where my family spent vacations. Every Monday night, when all the dads had left, the kids and moms would gather for a picnic around a driftwood bonfire. We'd sit on steamer blankets under the stars, eating fire-toasted s'mores and listening to the sounds of the ocean's waves.

Nonstick pan spray
About 2 cups confectioners' sugar
39 large marshmallows (15 for s'mores, 24 for serving)
3 whole graham crackers (6 squares)
3 1.55-ounce Hershey's milk chocolate bars, cut into 1-inch squares
2 tablespoons smooth peanut butter

Line the bottom of a 5 × 9-inch glass loaf pan with parchment paper, and then spray the bottom and sides with nonstick pan spray. Sift 2 tablespoons confectioners' sugar over the pan to liberally coat the bottom and sides.

Place 15 marshmallows in a microwave-safe bowl and microwave them in six 15-second increments, stirring after each, until the marshmallows are melted, about 1½ minutes total. Pour the marshmallows into the prepared pan and use a rubber spatula to smooth out the top. Cover the marshmallow layer with ¼ inch of confectioners' sugar. Refrigerate for 1 hour.

Place a small bowl of confectioners' sugar next to your work surface. Lift the parchment out of the loaf pan and set the marshmallow layer on your work surface. Use a 1-inch square cookie cutter to cut out 24 marshmallow squares, occasionally dipping the cutter into the confectioners' sugar to prevent it from sticking.

Break the graham cracker rectangles in half so you have 6 squares, and then break the squares into individual rectangles; you'll have 12 total. Use a serrated knife to gently saw each rectangle in half crosswise so you have 24 small squares.

Set an oven rack at the top position (about 3 inches from the broiler element) and heat the broiler to high. Place the graham cracker squares on an aluminum-foil-lined rimmed baking sheet. Place a chocolate square on each graham square, and cover the chocolate with a marshmallow square. Place the baking sheet in the oven and broil until the marshmallow is lightly browned, 15 to 30 seconds (watch your broiler closely, as heat intensity varies). Or, if you have a kitchen blowtorch, torch the marshmallows until browned.

Place a small dab of peanut butter on the bottom side of each of the remaining 24 marshmallows, and stick them to a serving tray, peanut butter side down. Balance the s'mores on top of the whole marshmallows, and serve.

MAKE AHEAD The marshmallow squares can be refrigerated in an airtight container for up to 1 week.

TIP Instead of melting the marshmallows and cutting them into squares, you can slice 6 large marshmallows crosswise into 4 thin rounds. Proceed building the s'mores as instructed.

bagel profiteroles

MAKES 2 DOZEN

Sometimes I like to take a commonplace savory item, in this case the bagel, and turn it into a dessert. The result is this humorous interpretation made with profiterole dough (like the shell of an éclair), vanilla pudding for the cream cheese, and mango or papaya slices for the lox.

1 2-ounce package vanilla pudding mix (not instant), such as Jell-O
2 cups all-purpose flour
½ teaspoon sugar
Pinch of table salt
4 tablespoons (½ stick) unsalted butter
2 large eggs, lightly beaten
1 papaya, peeled, halved, seeds removed, and thinly sliced (or 1 mango, peeled, pitted, and thinly sliced)
Fennel fronds, for serving (optional)

Make the pudding, following the package instructions. Cover the pudding directly with plastic wrap and refrigerate until serving.

Preheat the oven to 400°F.

Sift the flour, sugar, and salt together into a medium bowl, and set aside. In a large pot, melt the butter into ½ cup water over medium heat. Bring to a boil, remove the pot from the heat, and use a wooden spoon to stir the flour mixture into the hot water mixture until a dough ball forms, about 1 minute. Return the pan to the heat and beat vigorously for 2 minutes to release the steam. Slowly add the eggs and beat until a smooth paste forms, about 2 minutes. Scrape the paste into a pastry bag fitted with a medium-sized round tip.

Line a rimmed baking sheet with parchment paper, and pipe about 1 tablespoon of the paste into a 2-inch-wide, ½-inch-high ring, leaving a hole in the center (like a donut). Repeat with the remaining paste, leaving about 1½ inches between rings. Bake for 8 minutes. Then reduce the temperature to 325°F. and continue baking until light brown, 12 to 15 minutes. Turn off the oven and leave the baking sheet in the oven for 10 minutes to let the "bagels" dry out slightly. Then remove the baking sheet from the oven and set it aside to cool.

Slice each "bagel" almost all the way through horizontally, leaving it hinged on one side. Spread or pipe some vanilla pudding onto the bottom half, and top with a few papaya slices and a fennel frond (if using). Close the "bagel" and serve.

MAKE AHEAD The vanilla pudding can be refrigerated for up to 2 days before using.

The bagels can be baked and stored in an airtight container in a cool, dry place for up to 1 day.

The papaya can be sliced and refrigerated several hours before serving.

pecan tarts

MAKES 2 DOZEN

I have a sweet tooth, so sugary, caramely pecan tarts are right up my alley. As a one-bite dessert, they offer up the perfect amount of bliss. Add 2 tablespoons of bourbon to the filling for a spiked pecan tart.

FOR THE PECAN FILLING
¾ cup light corn syrup
5 tablespoons unsalted butter
1 cup (packed) light brown sugar
2 teaspoons vanilla extract
½ teaspoon table salt
3 large eggs, lightly beaten
24 pecan halves plus 2 cups toasted chopped pecans

FOR THE TARTS
24 baked pie shells (page 191)
¼ cup bittersweet chocolate chips (or finely chopped bittersweet chocolate)

pecan filling | Preheat the oven to 350°F.

In a 4-quart pot, bring the corn syrup, butter, and brown sugar to a boil over medium heat, stirring occasionally. Turn off the heat and stir in the vanilla and salt. Let cool for 5 minutes and then stir in the eggs. Add the pecan halves, stir to coat, and then strain through a fine-mesh sieve set over a medium bowl. Set the coated pecan halves aside, and stir the chopped pecans into the bowl containing the liquid.

tarts | Place the pie shells on a rimmed baking sheet. In a small microwave-safe bowl, melt the chocolate in the microwave in three or four 15-second increments, stirring after each, until no lumps remain. Using a pastry brush, coat each shell with melted chocolate. Set aside for 10 minutes to harden. Then fill each shell with about 1 tablespoon of the pecan filling. Place a pecan half on top of the tart. Bake the tarts until the filling only jiggles slightly when the pan is tapped, about 7 minutes. Remove from the oven and let cool completely.

serve | Remove the tarts from the tart pans, and serve.

MAKE AHEAD The tarts can be baked 2 days before serving. Cool completely, cover the baking sheet with plastic wrap, and refrigerate. Let the tarts sit out at room temperature for 20 minutes before serving.

OPEN BAR

Bourbon Pecans | Salty Edamame | Sgroppinos

Mint-tini | Cranberry-tini

Bubblegum-tini | Tini Trio: Tomato-tini, Lime-tini, Plum-tini

Pomegranate Mojito | Watermelon Margarita

Cucumber-Basil Margarita | Lemonade | Hot Mulled Cider

SOME OF MY MOST CREATIVE IDEAS ARE WOVEN around cocktails. The key to making them is to use fresh-squeezed juices, be it from a lime, watermelon, or cranberry. Fresh juice makes the most amazing-tasting and colorful drinks, embellished with alcohol or not. However, it's often the accessories that bring my drinks to a whole new level.

My forte with bars is to highlight the ingredients, turning them into a part of the presentation. I like to layer the raw ingredients used in making the cocktail, such as lime wheels, between the serving tray and a sheet of acrylic under the glasses. Sometimes I'll make an entire multicolored display out of carafes filled with various libations (see photo, page 210). I often instill a playful turn in the delivery—perhaps a margarita comes in a mini Patrón bottle, or mulled cider in a hollowed-out apple. The final result is often the same, with style winning out over function as cocktails *and* the bar become delicious objects of beauty.

bourbon pecans

MAKES 4 CUPS

From quality store-bought potato chips to home-made spiced pecans, bar snacks are a bonus component to any cocktail party.

4⅔ cups sugar
4 cups pecans
⅓ cup bourbon
1 tablespoon vegetable oil
1 tablespoon Worcestershire sauce
½ teaspoon bitters
⅔ teaspoon cayenne pepper
½ teaspoon chili powder
½ teaspoon coarse salt
½ teaspoon ground ginger
¼ teaspoon ground allspice
¼ teaspoon ground cardamom
¼ teaspoon ground cinnamon
¼ teaspoon ground coriander
¼ teaspoon freshly ground black pepper
¼ teaspoon freshly ground nutmeg
⅛ teaspoon ground cumin

Preheat the oven to 325°F.

In a medium saucepan, stir 4 cups of the sugar into 4 cups water and bring to a boil over medium-high heat, stirring occasionally until the sugar is completely dissolved. Add the pecans, boil for 5 minutes, and then strain through a fine-mesh sieve. Discard the sugar-water mixture.

In the same saucepan, stir the bourbon and ⅓ cup of the sugar over medium-high heat. Let the mixture simmer, stirring occasionally, until it's syrupy, about 3 minutes. Stir in the oil, Worcestershire, and bitters. Return the pecans to the pan and stir to coat them with the syrup. Remove from the heat and let the pecans soak up the liquid for 10 minutes.

Line a rimmed baking sheet with parchment paper. Spread the pecans evenly on the baking sheet, and toast them in the oven until they're dry and browned, 24 to 30 minutes, stirring every 10 minutes.

While the pecans are toasting, in a large bowl, whisk together the remaining ⅓ cup sugar and all the spices.

Remove the pecans from the oven, let them cool for 5 minutes, and then transfer them to the bowl of spices, tossing to coat them. Spread the pecans out on a baking sheet and let them cool completely.

Present the pecans in several small bowls grouped together or spread out among various tables.

MAKE AHEAD The pecans can be stored in an airtight container at room temperature for up to 12 days.

salty edamame

MAKES 1½ CUPS

If you can boil a saucepot of water, you can make this colorful, tasty, and nearly effortless bar snack. For a little salty crunch, try sprinkling the edamame with a flaky sea salt like fleur de sel or Maldon instead of using fine sea salt.

1 10-ounce bag frozen shelled edamame
Sea salt

Bring a large pot of water to a boil. Add the edamame and blanch them in the boiling water until they're tender, about 2 minutes. Drain through a fine-mesh sieve, shaking the sieve to ensure that the beans are as dry as possible.

Place the edamame in a medium bowl, sprinkle with sea salt, and toss to combine.

Portion the edamame into several small bowls and group them together onto one table or spread them out among many tables. Place a small spoon alongside the bowl for serving.

BYOB: Build Your Own Bar | It's not hard to set up a bar that's as beautiful as the drinks and hors d'oeuvres at any kind of party—fancy or casual. A bar is a great way to bring people together and get them mingling while also drawing them away from the spots where guests always seem to congregate, like the kitchen or a sitting area. A long table and a crisp, pressed tablecloth set a minimal foundation that shows off bottles, carafes filled with bright-hued mixers (using a small real fruit stopper is visually interesting and fun, see page 221), and bar snacks.

For the Mint-tini bar on page 214, we filled beaker-style carafes with the chilled Mint-tini mixture and displayed snacks, like artisanal potato chips, in glass boxes filled with kosher salt. Square glass containers are also a chic way to show off bottles of bubbly or white wine that need to be kept cold.

If you don't have space for a long table, that doesn't mean you need to forgo the bar idea completely. Instead, set up small tables for bottle service—a concept employed at the coolest nightclubs, where a chilled bottle of vodka gets delivered to your table in a Champagne-style bucket. We elevate the concept by using a tasteful lacquer box for chilling a few of your favorite bottles and having some juices available for a DIY cocktail station. Add a bucket of ice and cocktail glasses so guests can help themselves.

sgroppinos

MAKES I DOZEN DRINKS

A cross between a Champagne cocktail and a dessert, a fizzy Prosecco sgroppino has a frozen frothiness to it and is fantastic with limoncello liqueur drizzled over the top. We like to whisk large batches in an iced copper bowl right in front of guests—the action (and payoff) always draws a crowd. This is a semi-frozen drink that's best made to order or in small batches.

4 pints lemon sorbet
1½ cups chilled vodka
2¼ cups chilled Prosecco
Simple Syrup (page 215), if needed
¾ cup limoncello liqueur

Take the sorbet out of the freezer and let it sit at room temperature until it is soft but not melting, about 15 minutes. Scoop it into a large bowl and pour in the vodka. Whisk together until the mixture is smooth, and then whisk in the Prosecco. Taste, and adjust the sweetness with simple syrup if needed.

Divide among twelve frosted martini glasses, finish each with a drizzle of limoncello, and serve.

VARIATION

You can build a margarita bar by substituting watermelon sorbet for the lemon sorbet, silver tequila for the vodka, and Grand Marnier for the Prosecco. Festive alternatives for glasses are hollowed-out lemons (see page 228) or hollowed-out mini pineapples with the lids placed back on.

TIP Chilling glasses helps the drink stay cold and frothy. Place glasses in the freezer until they are frosty, or fill them with ice water and let them sit for a few minutes until they're chilled.

mint-tini

The citrusy Mint-tini is one of our most popular drinks. It has a very fresh, clean taste and a beautiful celadon-green color that is so summery. For a fizzy finish, make this with sparkling instead of still water. If you can't find Key limes, use small regular limes instead.

FOR THE MINT-TINI
3 cups fresh lime juice (from about 36 limes)
½ cup finely chopped fresh mint leaves
3 cups chilled vodka
3 cups still or sparkling water
3 cups chilled Simple Syrup (recipe follows)

FOR SERVING
4 Key limes, ends discarded, thinly sliced into wheels

mint-tini | Using a blender or food processor, purée the lime juice and mint leaves together for 1 minute. Add the vodka, still or sparkling water, and the simple syrup, and blend. Strain through a fine-mesh sieve into a large pitcher. Cover with plastic wrap and refrigerate until serving (if using sparkling water, serve immediately).

serve | Slice a slit in the edge of each of the Key lime wheels. Pour the Mint-tini into glasses, place a lime wheel on each rim, and serve.

MAKE AHEAD The lime juice can be squeezed and refrigerated 1 day in advance.

The mint leaves can be picked a day ahead of time, wrapped in a damp paper towel, and refrigerated.

simple syrup
MAKES 4 CUPS

Whether you're making a martini, a mojito, or a lemonade, simple syrup is a requisite ingredient. Made simply by boiling sugar and water, it effortlessly sweetens spiked and virgin concoctions. After turning off the heat, add herbs, spices, or citrus to infuse the simple syrup and bring another layer of flavor to the cocktail.

2 cups sugar
Citrus slices or zest strips, herbs, or spices (optional)

In a medium saucepan, stir the sugar into 2 cups water and bring to a boil over medium-high heat. Stir often until the sugar dissolves. Turn off the heat and set aside to cool (if infusing the simple syrup, add the citrus, herbs, or spices now). Pour the simple syrup into an airtight container and refrigerate until thoroughly chilled (if citrus, herbs, or spices were added, strain the syrup before refrigerating). Simple syrup can be refrigerated in an airtight container for up to 1 week.

cranberry-tini

MAKES 1 DOZEN DRINKS

I spend a lot of time on Nantucket, where cranberries are harvested from late September through November. It wasn't until a few years ago, though, that I tried fresh-pressed cranberry juice—it was like going from orange juice concentrate to fresh-squeezed. You can't believe how fabulous fresh cranberry juice is, and how different it tastes from the bottled kind in the supermarket.

Grated zest and juice of 6 oranges
5 cups fresh cranberries
½ cup sugar
3 cups chilled vodka
Ice
2 cups sparkling water

Place the orange zest and juice, 4 cups of the cranberries, the sugar, and 3¾ cups water in a food processor or blender, and purée. Strain through a fine-mesh sieve into a large pitcher. Stir in the vodka.

Thread the remaining cranberries on twelve cocktail swizzle sticks, 3 to a skewer. Fill twelve glasses with ice, and divide the cranberry mixture among the glasses, leaving enough room for a splash of sparkling water. Finish with the sparkling water, add the cranberry swizzle sticks, and serve.

MAKE AHEAD The cranberry mixture (without the vodka) can be refrigerated for up to 3 days.

The cranberry swizzle sticks can be made 1 day in advance. Store them, covered with water, in the refrigerator.

> **TIP** For a bold bar statement, dress your bar monochromatically. For the Cranberry-tini, I drape the table with a red tablecloth and dress the bar with red paper cocktail napkins, red glass candleholders, red candles, and a red glass bowl for ice. Use clear carafes to show off the matching hue of the drinks.

bubblegum-tini

MAKES 1 DOZEN DRINKS

Candy adds a fun and youthful feel to parties, whether it's incorporated into the décor or into a drink. In this bubblegum-inspired cocktail, we mix fresh orange juice with banana and melon liqueurs to give the martini the true fruity flavor of bubble-gum. We created this drink for an event at Dylan's Candy Bar in New York City and served them on trays filled with gumballs to bring the concept full circle.

6 cups fresh orange juice (from about 18 oranges)
3 cups chilled vanilla-flavored vodka
1 cup banana liqueur
¾ cup melon liqueur
Ice
1 orange, halved and thinly sliced (optional)
Gumballs, for serving

In a large pitcher, whisk together the orange juice, vodka, banana liqueur, and melon liqueur.

Fill twelve glasses with ice, and place an orange slice (if using) in each glass. Divide the Bubblegum-tini mixture among the glasses. Serve on a tray with shot glasses of gumballs.

> **TIP** Oversized swirl-candy lollipops make a great table decoration for the bar where the Bubblegum-tinis are served. Use a few vases and display them like flowers.

tini trio: tomato tini, lime-tini, plum-tini

MAKES 1 DOZEN OF EACH MARTINI

The vibrant colors of three fruit-infused martini variations presented together on a bar are dramatic, especially when bottled in attractive glass decanters to show off their amazing colors. The Lime-tini is bright and citrusy; the inky Plum-tini has an almost tealike quality; and the Tomato-tini is a playful herby spin on the Bloody Mary. A small piece of fruit acts as a stopper in each carafe while a bottle tag hung around the neck of the decanter adds a nice touch. For a virgin variation on any of these 'tinis, substitute sparkling water or a citrus-flavored soda for the alcohol.

FOR THE TOMATO-TINI
6 cups bottled tomato juice
6 fresh basil leaves
3 cups chilled vodka
1½ teaspoons coarse salt
Ice

FOR THE LIME-TINI
4 cups chilled Simple Syrup (page 215)
4 cups fresh lime juice (from about 48 limes)
4 cups chilled vodka
Ice

FOR THE PLUM-TINI
42 black or red plums (30 for the martini, 12 for serving)
½ cup sugar
2 cups chilled vodka
Ice

tomato-tini | In a blender or food processor, purée 2 cups of the tomato juice with the basil leaves. Pour the mixture into a large carafe or pitcher, and whisk in the remaining 4 cups tomato juice, the vodka, and the salt. Cover with plastic wrap and refrigerate until serving.

lime-tini | In a large carafe or pitcher, whisk together the simple syrup, lime juice, and vodka. Cover with plastic wrap and refrigerate until serving.

plum-tini | Halve and pit 30 plums. In a large pot, combine the halved plums, sugar, and 1 cup water over medium heat, and stir often until the liquid comes to a boil. Reduce the heat to medium-low and simmer until the plums are completely broken down, about 20 minutes. Strain the mixture through a fine-mesh sieve into a large carafe or pitcher. Stir in the vodka, cover with plastic wrap, and refrigerate until serving.

At serving time, halve, pit, and slice the remaining 12 plums. Cut a slit in the middle of each slice.

serve | Pour the drinks into a cocktail shaker filled with ice (or into a decanter, as shown opposite). Shake to chill, and then strain into martini glasses. Garnish Plum-tinis with a plum slice on the rim of each glass.

MAKE AHEAD The simple syrup can be refrigerated for up to 1 week.

pomegranate mojito

MAKES 1 DOZEN DRINKS

Pomegranates are at their seasonal peak during the wintertime, making this rich fuchsia cocktail a stunner at holiday parties and events. Since we use fresh lime juice in the cocktail, lime wheels are the perfect choice for garnishing the tray.

4 cups pomegranate juice
1 cup fresh lime juice (from about 12 limes)
1 cup chilled Simple Syrup (page 215)
2 cups fresh mint leaves
2 limes, ends discarded, cut into 12 wheels
2 cups light rum
Ice
Chilled club soda

Pour the pomegranate juice, lime juice, and simple syrup into a large pitcher. Stir in the mint leaves, cover with plastic wrap, and refrigerate overnight.

Strain the mixture through a fine-mesh sieve into a clean pitcher.

Decorate a tray with the lime wheels. Stir the rum into the mint-infused pomegranate mixture. Fill twelve glasses with ice, and divide the mojito among the glasses, leaving enough room for a splash of club soda. Finish with the club soda, and serve.

> **TIP** Decorate your bar with whole pomegranates stacked in glass or silver bowls. Alternate them with whole limes in a bowl on your bar for gorgeous pink-green contrast. Offer fresh pomegranate seeds in a small bowl with a small serving spoon as a bar snack.

watermelon margarita

MAKES 1 DOZEN DRINKS

Fresh watermelon juice is a wonderful margarita mixer and gives the cocktail a refreshing, summery look. This is an excellent choice for parties with guests of all ages, as the drink tastes just as delicious without the alcohol.

8 cups seedless watermelon chunks
1½ cups tequila, preferably Patrón Silver
¾ cup fresh lime juice (from about 9 limes)
¾ cup Grand Marnier
1½ cups chilled Simple Syrup (page 215)
Ice
12 small watermelon triangles with a slit cut into the
　rind, for serving

Purée the watermelon chunks in a blender or food processor until smooth, about 1 minute. Strain through a fine-mesh sieve into a large pitcher, and then stir in the tequila, lime juice, Grand Marnier, and simple syrup.

Fill twelve glasses with ice, and divide the margarita mixture among the glasses. Garnish each with a watermelon triangle, and serve.

MAKE AHEAD The watermelon juice can be made up to 3 days ahead; refrigerate it in an airtight container. Or it can be kept frozen for up to 3 weeks.

VARIATION

Substitute yellow watermelon instead of traditional red watermelon. Or make both and use them in side-by-side displays of either carafes or punch bowls. Use fresh watermelon balls in a jar as a bar snack.

cucumber-basil margarita

MAKES 1 DOZEN DRINKS

Cucumbers remind me of the cucumber fields that surrounded my grandparents' house on Long Island during the summertime. When juiced for drinks, cucumbers offer an incredible fresh flavor and a gorgeous celadon tint. Add tequila and basil and you get a genteel margarita that tastes as delicious as it looks.

10½ seedless (English) cucumbers
½ recipe chilled Simple Syrup (page 215) infused with
    15 fresh basil leaves
3 cups tequila, preferably Patrón Silver
2 cups fresh lemon juice (from about 12 lemons)
Ice

If you have a juicer, process 10 cucumbers through it to make cucumber juice. If you don't have a juicer, dice the cucumbers and use a blender or food processor to purée them with a little water. Strain the juice through a fine-mesh sieve into a pitcher. Stir in the basil simple syrup, tequila, and lemon juice.

Slice the remaining ½ cucumber into thin rounds, and cut a slit into the edge of each. Fill twelve glasses with ice, and divide the margarita mixture among the glasses. Perch a cucumber round onto the rim of each glass, and serve.

MAKE AHEAD The cucumber juice can be refrigerated up to 1 day in advance.

> **TIP** Try a cucumber theme for your next party. Serve cucumber tea sandwiches on trays at the bar and the Cucumber-Basil Margaritas alongside. Pimm's Cups made with Pimm's No. 1 liqueur and lemon sodas are great too (decorate the rim with a cucumber wheel). A green-and-white-checked bar cloth finishes the look.

lemonade

MAKES I DOZEN DRINKS

This is one of our most popular ways to serve a spe-cialty drink. The lemon "cup" with its lemon lid, paired with a yellow candy stick, is a great mix of the old-fashioned and the modern. Kids and adults love it—for the grown-ups, we often spike the lemonade with vodka. Of course the lemonade is just as deli-cious served in a tall glass, too. If you have a citrus press, you can save the fruit from making the lemon cups and use it for the 2 cups of lemon juice needed for the lemonade.

2 cups fresh lemon juice (from about 12 lemons)
4 cups chilled Simple Syrup (page 215)
12 large lemons
12 lemon candy sticks

In a large pitcher, stir together the lemon juice, 6 cups water, and the simple syrup. Taste, and add more water to dilute if needed. Cover with plastic wrap and refrigerate until chilled.

Cut a thin slice off the bottom of each lemon so it stands upright. Cut off the top of the lemon. Use a paring knife to slice around the fruit, separating it from the rind and being careful not to cut through the bottom of the lemon. Use a grapefruit spoon to remove the fruit from the rind, creating a hollow cup.

Divide the lemonade among the lemon cups. Finish with a candy stick and a straw, and perch the lids atop.

MAKE AHEAD The lemonade can be refrigerated for up to 2 days.

VARIATIONS

Make strawberry or raspberry lemonade simply by adding 1 cup of strawberry or raspberry purée to the lemonade recipe. Freeze the lemonade in a popsicle mold for a dessert twist on the drink (see page 181 for a DIY popsicle serving tray).

hot mulled cider

MAKES I DOZEN DRINKS

When I was in college in Burlington, Vermont, I regularly hiked through the Green Mountains to take full advantage of the peak foliage season. Apple cider was in abundance at nearly every general store and farm stand. I drew on these memories to create a classic apple cider. We serve it in a hollowed apple cup that elevates it from farm-stand Dixie cup to a modern party cocktail. The apples are so beautiful on their own that they are a natural choice for serving the cider (of course a nice mug works, too!). If you decide to spike the cider, it increases the yield to about 14 servings.

FOR THE CIDER
9 cups apple cider
1 orange, sliced into ¼-inch-thick rounds
1 lemon, sliced into ¼-inch-thick rounds
1 cinnamon stick
2 whole cloves
1 whole star anise pod (optional)

FOR SERVING
12 small Gala or McIntosh apples
2¼ cups dark rum (optional)
12 cinnamon sticks

mulled cider | In a large pot, bring the apple cider, orange slices, lemon slices, cinnamon stick, cloves, and star anise (if using) to a simmer over medium heat. Simmer for 20 minutes, and then strain through a fine-mesh sieve into a large clean pot.

serve | Cut a small slice off the bottom of each apple so it stands upright. Cut the top third off the apples and set the tops aside. Using a paring knife, carve the centers out of the apples, going 1 inch deep and leaving at least a ¼-inch border around the edges. Use a grapefruit spoon to scoop the fruit out of the apples, creating a cup shape. Be careful not to puncture the sides or bottoms of the apples.

Warm the cider over medium heat (add the rum now, if using) and divide it among the prepared apple cups. Serve each with a cinnamon stick and the apple top as a lid.

MAKE AHEAD The apple cups can be refrigerated for several hours before serving. Place them on a baking sheet and squeeze lemon juice over all the cut surfaces to prevent them from browning.

THEMES + MENUS

IF THERE IS ONE THING I HAVE LEARNED DURING many years of catering parties, it's that a great party is never just about the food—it's about the spectacle of presentation, too. Customizing trays, paper goods, and even the food itself (branding irons come in handy for this!) is a way to honor the theme of the party, whether it's a person (for a birthday, an anniversary, or a shower) or an occasion (like a holiday party). In this chapter, you'll discover some creative ways to serve the hors d'oeuvres and drinks featured throughout the book. Most of the images are easy to duplicate—they just require a dash of extra effort and ingenuity, and your own twist, of course. Along with the ideas are some suggested menus appropriate for the occasion. These are in no way set in stone; they are simply a reflection of compositions that are hits with my guests. Feel free to make your own changes and create a menu that speaks to your favorite flavors, dishes, and ideas.

customizing is everything

selecting a theme

A theme is often your best road map to creating memorable components of a party that extend beyond the food. You can go all out or keep the theme subtle. An example of the former is a *Wizard of Oz* birthday party we catered. We made yellow brick trays for serving, and there was a yellow brick road for guests to wander down. We even cut Toto-shaped dogs out of smoked salmon for hors d'oeuvres (see page 242). Sometimes it takes only a few subtle touches to create an ambience. For a sophisticated Asia-inspired party, we filled the bases of drink trays with chic black river rocks, strung gold coins on threads and attached them to serving trays so they dangled and swayed, and decorated the bar tables with lanky stems of bamboo in tall cylindrical glass vases.

Themes aren't the only way to customize a party. You can also personalize by offering fun messages inspired by the guest of honor tucked into fortune cookies or by commemorating the date by printing it on frites cones. Another technique I like to use is to layer printed images, such as ticket stubs or even real flowers or ingredients (lemon or lime wheels, herb sprigs) between the surface of a tray and an acrylic sheet that fits perfectly on top. Fresh lemonade looks that much more inviting when served on top of cheery daisies that are pressed between the tray and clear acrylic, and imagine the impact of flutes of Champagne served on top of Bordeaux-colored chrysanthemums at a holiday party! Images that celebrate the guest of honor—perhaps highlighting his or her favorite sport, first initial, or age—are always a great idea. Illustrations or stamps of little baby feet featured on a tray are adorable for baby showers and first birthday parties.

creating a memorable menu

Choosing a menu to suit the theme or the guest of honor is a must, as is coordinating the right number of hors d'oeuvres to accommodate the length of the party. You want enough food going around to keep your guests satisfied while not overwhelming them with options. Five or six different types of hors d'oeuvres is a good number for a one-hour event at home. For two hours, I up the ante to ten different hors d'oeuvres. If a party stretches across a mealtime or goes beyond two hours, I like to include a few dessert hors d'oeuvres. Desserts are a great crowd-pleaser and also subconsciously signal to your guests that the party is winding down. For parties that extend into the night, I suggest ending the event with a breakfast hors d'oeuvre like Bagels and Lox (page 157), Oatmeal Crème Brûlée (page 169), or Scrambled Eggs and Bacon (page 159).

the perfect menu

A balanced menu is a perfect menu. Here are some pointers to keep in mind when you're ready to build your party set list:

- Plan on a minimum of four hors d'oeuvres per person per hour (for a party with 20 guests, you'd need 80 hors d'oeuvres). That said, we offer up to 14 hors d'oeuvres per guest per hour for hour-long parties before celebratory dinners (like a wedding).
- Offer an equal split of vegetarian, beef, poultry, and seafood options.
- Serve a good balance of rich bites (Lobster Rolls, Frites, Mac and Cheese Canapés) with light ones (Tuna Tartare Plantain Cones, Vegetable Spring Rolls).
- Balance warm hors d'oeuvres with cold ones.

winter celebrations

I LIKE TO CREATE a theme reflective of the holiday by dressing and trimming our trays. Silver sleigh bells dangling from tiered tray corners are old-world fabulous in a Currier & Ives way. We simply slide thread through the bells and tape them to the tray corners. You can also fill transparent glass bowls to the brim with sleigh bells—the light reflects off them and creates an incredibly atmospheric space.

Flat, shiny items like metallic snowflakes can be casually strewn across a dining room table or used to decorate serving trays. Silver and gold are pretty, as are metallic reds and blues. Small plaid bows and red-and-green-striped ribbons look adorable on tiered trays. Simply glue them onto the edges with a glue gun or use double-sided tape. Red-striped peppermints and snowflake-emblazoned take-out boxes and frites cones are other embellishments we like.

To take some of the prep time out of holiday entertaining, I like to keep liquor stored in beautiful decanters and bottles. Simple hand-written labels on heavy-stock cards, tied around decanter necks with raffia, denote what is within. Keep a few carafes handy for displaying mixers and ice water. Thin rounds of birch logs can be used as trays, and a beautiful pressed linen cloth, or even more rustic burlap, creates a beautifully low-key presentation that can be a welcome break from the customary holiday sparkle.

MENU
UNTRADITIONAL THANKSGIVING DINNER

A spread of miniature holiday bites is my favorite way to celebrate this most food-driven holiday.

Cranberry-tinis (page 216)
Butternut Squash Lollipops (page 89)
Twice-Baked Stuffed Potatoes (page 30)
Sweet Onion Canapés with Mashed Peas (page 29)
Turkey Canapés with Stuffing and Cranberry Relish (page 130)
Pecan Tarts (page 205)
Caramel Lady Apples with Chocolate Ganache Cores (page 197)
Hot Mulled Cider (page 231)

MENU
NEW YEAR'S EVE PARTY

Mini bottles of alcohol—those little single-serving bottles you get on an airplane are available in liquor stores—convey a party atmosphere. You can do this with Patrón bottles and quesadillas (see page 74) or splits of Champagne (each split yields one fourth of a standard-sized bottle). After midnight, when the party is winding down, I like to send out one or two breakfast items to re-energize guests.

Mint-tinis (page 215)
Buckwheat Blinis, Caviar, and Vodka (page 60)
Lobster-Potato Petit Fours (page 115)
Stuffed Mushrooms (page 111)
Foie Gras Truffles (page 109)
Sgroppinos (page 212)
Baked Alaskas (page 185)
Scrambled Eggs and Bacon (page 159)
Oatmeal Crème Brûlée (page 169)

kids and showers

Showers, whether for a baby or a bride, are about celebrating new beginnings, so these events should be lighthearted and whimsical. For baby showers, I like to stagger rubber duckies between silver demitasse spoonfuls of Mac and Cheese (you could even use boxed mac and cheese to pull off this look). Sometimes I alternate a forkful of Spaghetti and Meatballs with the mac and cheese to create a truly comforting party platter. Scans of baby-food jar labels and iconic images (like the Gerber baby or baby footprints) are fun to use as tray liners or lacquered onto thick backings to use as coasters.

When it comes to bridal showers, remember that the honoree will probably be opening gifts while everyone else is perched on chairs and watching. It's important to keep the food easy to eat and bite-sized so no one is distracted from the main event. I like to start the shower by serving the cocktail that the couple drank during their first date or when they got engaged. Decorate the tray with the bride-to-be's new monogram to bring the idea full circle.

A child's birthday party is all about fun—from the decorations to the drinks and food. Food served in miniature is truly ideal for kids, giving them just the right bite size to satiate their hunger. Fluttery silklike butterflies can take flight as they work their way up a tiered pink tray of lunchtime treats. (To duplicate the look, fix three wood disks together using wood dowels and a drill, then paint the tray pink and glue on silk butterflies purchased from a craft supply store.)

MENU
BABY SHOWER

When it comes to baby showers, I like to indulge the mom-to-be and her guests. I pull out all of the crave-worthy foods, like fried chicken, mac and cheese, and other "lighter" crowd pleasers like BLTs. Color-coded cotton candy (pink for a girl, blue for a boy) is always a hit, too.

BRIDAL SHOWER

A bridal shower can be a blur of excitement, so I like to serve food that will add to the energy of the day. Often clients think of a standard lunch buffet, but when I suggest the idea of bite-sized hors d'oeuvres, they absolutely love it. Since showers often happen during brunch time, it's fun to mix in a few breakfast bites.

Cucumber-Basil Margaritas (page 227)
Bagels and Lox (page 157)
Vegetable Spring Rolls (page 127)
Ham, Egg, and Cheese (page 160)
Butternut Squash Lollipops (page 89)
Crab in Potato Cones (page 99)
Potted Shrimp (page 122)
Caprese Tea Sandwiches (page 21)
Spicy Chicken "Fortune Cookies" (page 65)
Chipwich Lollipops (page 182)
Limoncello Popsicles (page 181)

KIDS PARTY

Kids love recognizable food, and classic American dishes never fail to please. Combine these two concepts into miniature hors d'oeuvres and their eyes will absolutely light up when they see bite-sized pizzas headed their way! Pint-sized hors d'oeuvres seem tailor-made for kids because they're so fun and easy to eat.

Peace of Pizza (page 19)
Mac and Cheese Canapés (page 25)
Root Beer and Pretzels (page 78, substituting root beer)
Grilled Cheese (page 53)
Chicken-Parmesan Lollipops (page 91)
Cheeseburgers and Fries (page 42)
Classic Pigs in Blankets (page 121)
Rice Krispy Canapés with Yogurt and Berries (page 155)
Milk and Cookies (page 178)
Fluffernutters (page 194)

celebrations for four-legged friends

PEOPLE *LOVE* THEIR DOGS and treat them as family. Dogs are dressed up and taken everywhere—to the hair salon, to dinner, shopping. Why not throw a party in their honor? For unique parties like these, I take an existing recipe—like the smoked salmon pigs with wasabi caviar "blankets" (page 121)—and give it a twist by using a Scottie dog–shaped cookie cutter instead of pig-shaped one. A strategically placed stripe of wasabi caviar becomes the dog's collar, and there you have it: Scottie in a Blanket. To bring it to the next level, I present them on a Tiffany-blue tray with real dog collars as tray decorations! Dog tags printed with the dogs' names are also a great way to personalize the party; you can use them to decorate tables and even trays. If your guest of honor is a Dalmatian, you could even wrap the frites cones with black-and-white polka-dot gift wrap.

MENU
DOG PARTY

The key here is imagery. All you need is a few cookie cutters and a little imagination to turn hors d'oeuvres into dog-themed ones! A few doggie biscuits for the guest of honor is a nice touch, too.

Dog Bone–Shaped Grilled Cheese Sandwiches
   (page 53; pictured opposite)
Scottie in a Blanket (page 121; pictured opposite)
Hot Dogs (page 45)
Sweet Frites (page 174)
Milk and Dog Biscuit–Shaped Cookies (page 178)

a dinner party for six

FOR A CLASSIC SIT-DOWN dinner party, I draw inspiration from the Minis Go Main chapter. There is no reason to sacrifice wit and whimsy just because the gathering is more traditional in nature. It's fun to stick to a conventional route of bread-soup-salad-entrée-dessert and then shake things up by the way the food is presented. Instead of a bread basket, offer an entire miniature loaf of challah on its own tiny cutting board. To keep with the theme, serve dessert on wood boards, too.

MENU
MINIS GO MAIN

Presented in slightly larger serving sizes, appetizers can surely be tweaked for a dinner party.

Mini Challah Loaves (page 112)
Pea Soup and Caprese Salad (page 149)
BBQ Chicken (page 142)
Corn Cakes (page 150)
Caramel Lady Apples with Chocolate Ganache Cores
   (page 197)
Hot Mulled Cider (page 231)

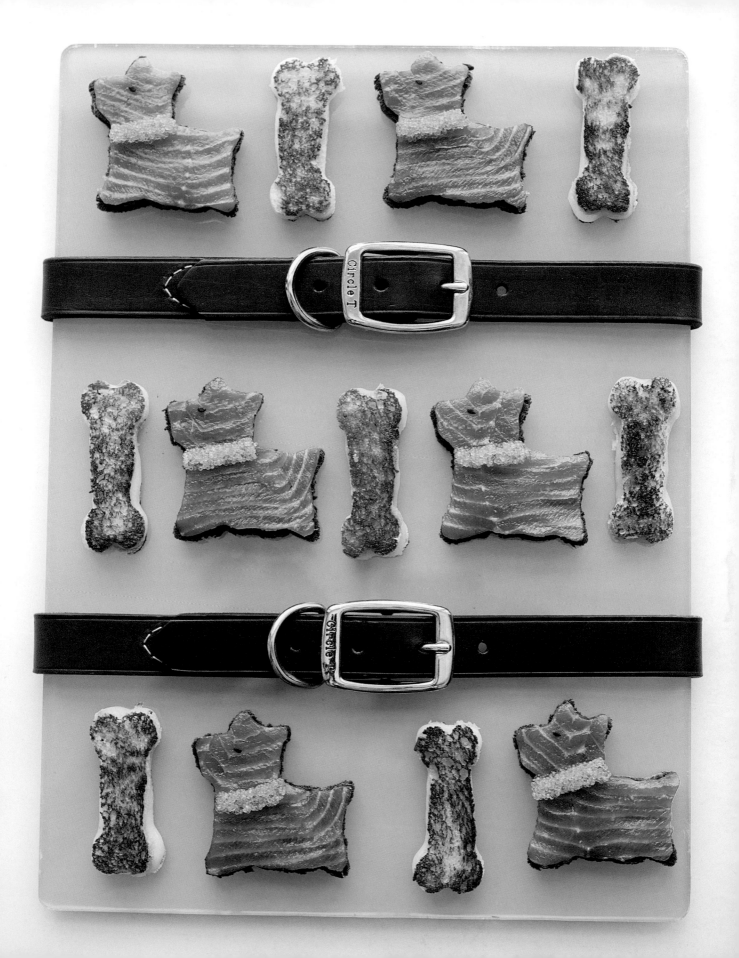

big dates

At milestone events such as engagements, weddings, birthdays, and graduations, there are often guests from various backgrounds, so you want to serve food with wide appeal. Comfort food is ideal as it pleases people of all backgrounds and culinary tastes. Since guests often travel to get to the event (and expect to be fed heartily), plan on serving lots of hors d'oeuvres. Fourteen per guest is not out of the ordinary! Also plan on having a cocktail hour before the mains (whether in mini form or standard size). Guests expect as much at these landmark occasions.

For presentation, it's all about personalization. Inscribe the date of the event on tags and hang them from decanters filled with cocktail mixers and premixed martinis. Personalize stickers with a monogram or picture and adhere them to Chinese take-out containers. Ask guests to send in favorite inside jokes shared with the guest of honor to tuck into fortune cookies. You can even brand barbecued chicken with the honoree's initials!

MENU
POST-WEDDING BRUNCH

Introducing a few fanciful elements from an evening menu gives a brunch a dressier tone.

Sgroppinos (page 212)
Fried Clams and Bloody Marys (page 62)
Deviled Quail Eggs (page 125)
Foie Gras Truffles (page 109)
Pancake Stacks (page 162)
French Toast (page 165)
Caviar Cones (page 102)
Pigs in Blankets, Two Ways (page 121)
Rice Krispy Canapés with Yogurt and Berries (page 155)
Sugar Donuts (page 166)
Bagel Profiteroles (page 202)

MENU
ENGAGEMENT COCKTAIL PARTY

Offer fun finger foods and great cocktails to get the party going and friends mingling. I love using Tiffany-blue trays and white ribbon bows for engagement parties.

Martini Bar, featuring the Tini Trio (page 220)
Fish Tacos (page 72) and Margaritas in mini Patrón bottles
Vegetable Spring Rolls (page 127)
Tuna Tartare Plantain Cones (page 96)
Caviar Spoons and Vodka (page 59)
Lobster-Potato Petit Fours (page 115)
Mango-Shrimp Lollipops (page 84)
Artichoke Lollipops (page 83)
Chicken Noodle Soup (page 41)
Spicy Chicken "Fortune Cookies" (page 65)
Fried Clams and Bloody Marys (page 62)
Short Rib Burgers (page 140)

MENU
BIRTHDAY OR GRADUATION PARTY

This party is all about the person of the hour. It should feature his or her favorite foods and drinks. These are mine!

Fried Chicken (page 67) and Cuba Libres (rum and Coke) in mini soda bottles
Fish Tacos (page 72) and Margaritas in mini Patrón bottles
Caviar Spoons and Vodka (page 59)
Pigs in Blankets, Two Ways (page 121)
Chicken Nori Cigarettes (page 105)
Grilled Cheese (page 53)
Cheeseburgers and Frites (page 42)
Spicy Chicken "Fortune Cookies" (page 65)
Cotton Candy Lollipops (page 190)
Mint-tinis (page 215)

summer parties

DURING THE SUMMERTIME, most hosts want to take their parties outdoors. The setting impacts the menu as much as the theme and occasion do. If I'm catering a garden party in a lush setting, the menu will be quite different than if it's a beach party or a dinner on a boat. At these more casual parties, I find that guests seem to come and go at their leisure. Jump on the laid-back vibe by presenting stationary displays of hors d'oeuvres that allow partygoers to take what they like when they want. Just remember to keep refilling the trays and refreshing ice buckets and cocktail mixers when the offerings grow slim.

A key tip for outdoor entertaining is to keep the food shaded. Umbrella tables are a huge help. Also, avoid quick-to-spoil items that require ice to keep cool, like sushi and chocolate desserts or cakes with buttercream. Additionally, people like to eat room-temperature or cool foods in the summertime (making the actual party preparation easier, since those items can be made in advance and held at room temperature or refrigerated until serving). Save the piping-hot hors d'oeuvres for winter events.

I like coordinating the outdoor elements with the hors d'oeuvres. I use wooden platters for the food and handled buckets for chilling bottles at the bar. Galvanized pails are great for stocking with ice and fun bottles of soda. Bright and festive linens are essential.

For these casual affairs, I often present a whole meal on a tray. An example is the red, white, and blue acrylic tower (opposite) that presents a burger alongside a strawberry-rhubarb pie and a cream soda float (simply ice cream and cream soda in a tall glass). Miniature flags are a must for Fourth of July gatherings.

MENU

SUMMER HOLIDAY PARTY OR BARBECUE

A summer party is all about avoiding stress and enjoying the good life. I like to break out the buffet so guests can help themselves. This can be easy and breezy.

Lemonade (page 228)
Savory Buffet: Hot Dogs (page 45), Lobster Rolls (page 48), Classic Shrimp Cocktail Lollipops (page 84)
Sweet Buffet: Strawberry-Rhubarb Pies (page 191), Sugar Donuts (page 166), PB and Js (page 187)

MENU

ALFRESCO GARDEN PARTY

Elegant and casual come head-to-head at an alfresco event. Hors d'oeuvres that speak of the garden are a perfect match.

Cheese and Wine (page 56)
Watermelon-Mint Lollipops (page 87)
Quesadillas and Margaritas (page 74)
Caprese Tea Sandwiches (page 21)
Grilled Vegetables in Plantain Cones (page 100)
Tuna Cheesesteaks (page 22)
Corn Soup and Bacon (page 76)
Sweet Onion Canapés with Mashed Peas (page 29)
Potted Shrimp (page 122)

kosher parties

THROWING A PARTY that adheres to kosher dietary guidelines need not be daunting. I recently opened a uniquely kosher version of Peter Callahan Catering so guests with kosher dietary needs can enjoy the same type of fun and stylish hors d'oeuvres as our non-kosher clients and be confident that the parameters of kosher dining are being upheld.

There are three types of kosher parties: a dairy party, where food with dairy is allowed but anything made with meat is not; a meat party, where meat is allowed but any food made with dairy is not; or a parve party, which includes foods made without meat *or* dairy. According to kosher principles, the food should also be prepared using pots, pans, and utensils that fall in line with the dietary restrictions of the party (so for a dairy party, you wouldn't make a vegetarian soup in a pot that was once used to make a soup with meat) and should be served on plates and with flatware that also falls within the parameters of dairy, meat, or parve. No recipes can have pork or shrimp, both proteins strictly prohibited by people who follow a kosher diet. Adding a kosher wine to the menu is a nice touch.

MENU

A DAIRY PARTY

A dairy-based party is mostly vegetarian with some fish (it must have scales—no shellfish). The key here is to craft a menu that is satisfying even though beef, lamb, and chicken aren't served. I like to include sandwiches, cheese-based dishes, and recipes that call for mushrooms, which have a great meaty quality.

Mini Challah Loaves (page 112)
Artichoke Lollipops (page 83)
Butternut Squash Lollipops (page 89)
Mac and Cheese Canapés (page 25)
Tomato Soup and Grilled Cheese (page 53)
Stuffed Mushrooms (page 111)
Tuna Tartare Plantain Cones (page 96)
Vegetable Lasagnas (page 38)
Bagel Profiteroles (page 202)

MENU

A MEAT PARTY

Balancing rich meat dishes with lighter ones is the trick to pulling off a meat party. Of course, a few vegetable-based items (made without butter, cheese, or milk) are a welcome addition.

Mini Challah Loaves (page 112), made with parve soy milk and margarine
Beef and Beer (page 70), substituting kosher rib-eye steaks for the filet
Vegetable Spring Rolls (page 127), using kosher spring roll wrappers
Pheasant Under Glass (page 118)
Chicken Noodle Soup (page 41)
Grilled Vegetables in Plantain Cones (page 100)
Lamb and Mint Pesto Lollipops (page 95)
Cotton Candy Lollipops (page 190)
Limoncello Popsicles (page 181)

when dessert is theme enough

I LIKE TO PRESENT classic and iconic desserts in stylish ways. This pleases everyone, from kids to grown-ups. Served after a meal, dessert instantly ramps up the energy of a party and leaves guests with another memorable takeaway that they'll talk about for weeks after the party ends. Like the tiered presentation of Milk and Cookies (page 236)—can anything be more simple or stylish?

I have many clients who say, "Peter, just skip it all—let's go straight to dessert!" And why not? Dessert is often one of the highlights of a meal, so why not make it the focus of one? It's a good idea to offer one fruit item and at least one chocolate one. The rest is up to you.

Instead of a celebratory cake, I like an unexpected tiered tray of cupcakes, Milk and Cookies, Caramel Lady Apples, and even Fluffernutters. A really big tray makes an especially strong showing—the one shown on page 236 is three feet high, so combined with the height of the table, it's a whopping five feet tall!

If the party is not being held in a traditional setting, I like to pull out all the stops when it comes to passing out the sweets. A stilt walker with Cotton Candy Lollipops in her pants pockets (see page 245) is a perfect example. A more low-key yet just as poignant offering is to present the lollipops as an edible centerpiece or hand them to guests as a favor when they leave.

One of my favorite ways to unveil dessert is by bringing it out with its very own fireworks display—sparklers! Baked Alaskas (page 185), cupcakes, and even pies instantly have a celebratory quality when they're topped with a sparkler. Use them to punctuate any kind of party or to add a touch of glitter and glam to the end of a night.

MENU
DESSERT PARTY

Chipwich Lollipops (page 182)
Fluffernutters (page 194)
Chocolate Ice Cream "Burgers" (page 175)
Sweet Frites (page 174)
Fudgesicles (page 173)
Watermelon-Mint Lollipops (page 87)
Strawberry-Rhubarb Pies (page 191)
Sugar Donuts (page 166)

RESOURCES

My team and I spend a lot of time searching out the perfect platters, mini mugs, and serving ware, not to mention key ingredients like wasabi caviar and truffles, that absolutely make a dish. This list details the sources I turn to when I need something to make a party or hors d'oeuvre special.

EQUIPMENT AND SERVING WARE

Acrylic containers, ice buckets, and sheets
www.clearlyacrylic.com
877-360-4163

Branding irons
www.steakbrands.com
800-985-5358

Cannoli tubes
JB Prince
36 E. 31st Street
New York, NY 10016
www.jbprince.com
800-473-0577

Chinese take-out boxes, ceramic soupspoons, and sake cups
www.asianideas.com
877-407-9259

www.orientaltrading.com
800-875-8480

Cookie cutters and pastry tips
www.pastrysampler.com
760-440-9171

Spoon-shaped cookie cutters
www.thecookiecuttershop.com
360-652-3295

Mini cups, mugs, and glasses
www.giantpartystore.com
866-244-1169

Plastic 1½-inch-high shot glasses
www.orientaltrading.com
800-875-8480

Small wine glasses with stems
www.ikea.com/us
800-434-IKEA

Glass domes and matching trays
www.crateandbarrel.com
800-967-6696

Hibachi grills
www.chefsresource.com

www.potterybarn.com
888-779-5176

Mini loaf pans
2¼ x 11¾-inch loaf pan (by Ateco)
www.webstaurantstore.com
717-392-7472
3¼ x 5¾-inch loaf pan (by Chicago Metallic)
www.kitchenkapers.com
800-455-5567

Lollipop sticks and popsicle sticks
www.acmoore.com
888-ACMOORE

Mandoline (we like the Benriner brand)
www.surlatable.com
800-243-0852

Pallet holder for cones
www.pastryitems.com
443-417-8854

Waffle cone maker (PetitCone Express model 836 by Chef's Choice)
www.chefsresource.com
866-765-CHEF

INGREDIENTS

Caramel apple kit (by Concord Foods)
www.wegmans.com
800-WEGMANS

Caviar
American paddlefish caviar
www.paramountcaviar.com
800-99-CAVIAR

Wasabi caviar
www.markys.com
800-522-8427

Foie gras and truffles (fresh and preserved)
www.markys.com
800-522-8427

Grape leaves (canned)
www.kalustyans.com
800-352-3451

Riccia pasta (we like the Rustichella d'Abruzzo brand)
www.manicaretti.com
800-799-9830

Smoked sea salt
www.saltworks.us
800-353-7258

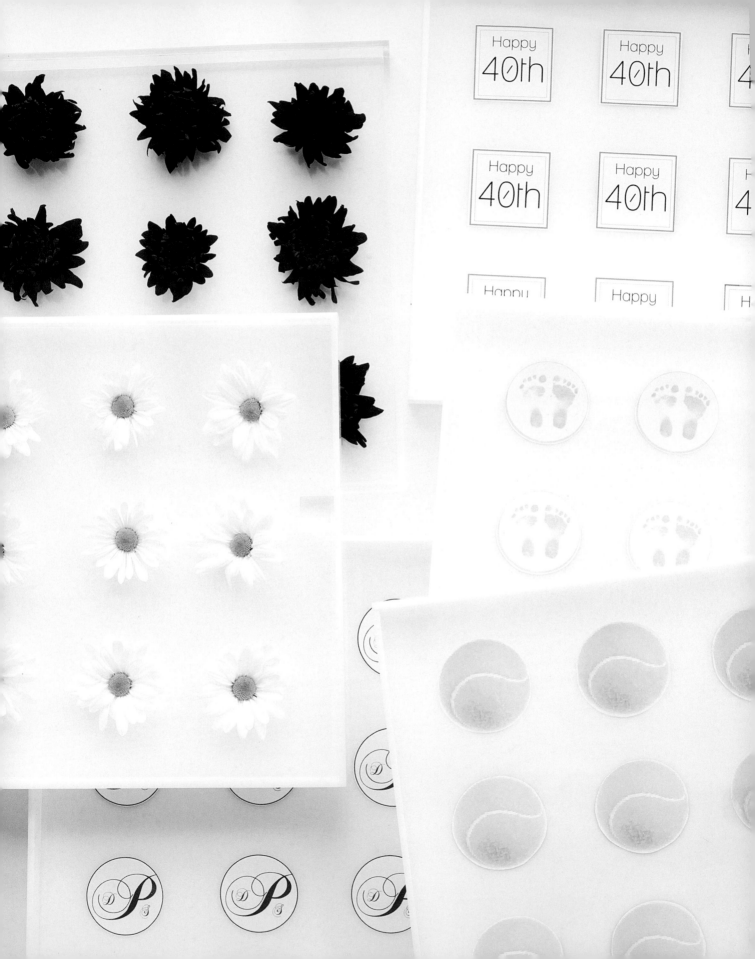

ACKNOWLEDGMENTS

FIRST I WANT TO THANK Beth, Shania, Jana, and Rob, who help make this party happen every day. We have worked and had fun together for many years, and they are a big part of all we do.

I would also like to thank my editor, Emily Takoudes, of Clarkson Potter, my writer, Raquel Pelzel, and the photographer Con Poulos.

Martha Stewart and Kevin Sharkey were both instrumental. Even before its inception, every time I saw Martha, she'd ask, "When are you doing a book, Peter?" Thanks for helping every step of the way to make this a reality.

There are many other important people I work with who have contributed. They are too many to name, but they have helped over the years to produce all of our events. Special thanks to Michelle Wong for prop styling and more and to Alexa Mulvill for their contributions to this book.

INDEX